Advanced Commodity Spread Trading

ADVANCED COMMODITY SPREAD TRADING

By Harold Goldberg

WINDSOR BOOKS, BRIGHTWATERS, N.Y.

Published by Windsor Books
P. O. Box 280
Brightwaters, N.Y. 11718

Manufactured in the United States of America

CAVEAT: It should be noted that all commodity trades, patterns, charts, systems, etc., discussed in this book are for illustrative purposes only and are not to be construed as specific advisory recommendations. Further note that no method of trading or investing is foolproof or without difficulty, and past performance is no guarantee of future performance. All ideas and material presented are entirely those of the author and do not necessarily reflect those of the publisher or bookseller.

Acknowledgements

My sincere thanks and appreciation go to Mr. Donald Lambert, President, Lambert Programming Service, for his incisive critique.

Sincere thanks and appreciation, as well, are extended to the highly skilled, experienced, and gifted editor and typist, Debba Rofheart, without whose diligence, this book would not have become a reality.

Mr. Harold Goldberg has had extensive experience covering three decades as a researcher, writer, advisor and account executive. His book is the result of over 30 years of trial and error toward finding the optimum method of anticipating futures spread movements.

"Virtue has never been as respected as money"
Mark Twain

"—and making money is what this book is all about"

Harold Goldberg

Table of Contents

Graphs

Introduction

This book was written for both the experienced spread trader and the commodity trader who has to date shied away from spread trading because of limited knowledge about spreads. The experienced spread trader will find a distinct improvement upon the conventional spread charts which many believe to be lacking in effectiveness, while the less experienced trader will find a wealth of knowledge about spreads which will hopefully lead him to embrace spread trading. Lastly, I believe those who do not consider spreads as a profitable trading vehicle are in for a pleasant revelation.

Prologue

This book on profitable spread trading uses the twin line spread graph technique which is an approach I personally devised. The book took me almost a year to write, while the technique itself was developed through over three decades of experience "on the firing line."

To this point in time spread graphs have consisted of one line delineating the closing spread difference between contracts. These traditional spread graphs do not lend themselves to consistently obtaining good entry and exit signals. A one line spread graph is, by its construction, one dimensional. Not only are they difficult to trade, but they also are of limited help in obtaining propitious stop and trailing stop differentials. On the other hand, the twin line spread graph:

1. Is two dimensional.
2. Highlights, in bold relief, entry and reverse signals.
3. Illuminates trend reversals.
4. Avoids sideway moving spreads.
5. Dramatically reduces whipsaws.
6. Keeps the spread trader out of break-even spreads.

Chapter 1

The Language of Spreads

Whenever possible, throughout this book, I have opted to use plain English. However, a few technical terms were unavoidable. Most of the nomenclature used by spreaders will be covered in this chapter. Other terms will be explained as they crop up in subsequent chapters.

BULL SPREADS

A Bull spread is one in which the near month is expected to gain relative to the distant month of the same commodity (i..e.—long Dec. 1983 Corn/short May 1984 Corn). When the same commodity forms a spread, it is called an intra-commodity spread.

The second type of Bull spread involves different, but related, futures contracts (i.e.—Dec. 1983 Wheat vs. Dec. 1983 Corn). In this spread you expect wheat to gain on corn. To correctly label this trade, you would go long the wheat and short the corn. This spread is called an inter-commodity spread.

The third type of Bull spread involves the same commodity traded on different futures exchanges. Wheat, for example, is traded on the Chicago Board of Trade (CBT), the Kansas City Board of Trade (KC) and the Minneapolis Grain exchange. The spread is composed of going long wheat on one exchange and shorting wheat on a different exchange. This spread is called an inter-exchange spread, or inter-market spread.

BEAR SPREAD

A bear spread is the exact reverse of a bull spread. The names of the types of spreads do not change. In an intra-commodity spread, you are looking for the near month to lose relative to the distant month. When trading an inter-market spread, you expect the first futures contract to lose relative to the distant month. And when trading an inter-exchange spread, you expect the futures contract listed on the first exchange to lose relative to the same futures contract traded on the second exchange. Remember though, regardless of a spread's component contracts, the spread is always either a bull or a bear spread. The principle is the same (i.e.—one against the other).

SPREAD SEASONALITY

Spreads in general, have a seasonal tendency to move higher or lower during different calendar months. The grain and meat spreads have a high correlation to seasonality. The grains' seasonality is influenced by the planting and harvesting periods. The meats' seasonality is influenced by gestation and maturation periods (the time that it takes for cows and hogs to reach slaughter weights).

Later we will be looking at those months when spreads make their lows and highs. I call these time periods "The Monthly Turning Points (MTP's)." I've also found some spreads to make double tops and/or bottoms in different months. These, too, will be studied.

CONTRA-SEASONAL MOVES

There are *no* certainties in the study of seasonal characteristics of spreads. They do, by and large, have a high probability of conforming, but exceptions are numerous. Expected monthly turning points often do not materialize. A spread may continue well past the month in which it was supposed to turn in an opposite direction. This is called a contra-seasonal move. The astute spreader will take advantage of them when they occur.

Contra-seasonal trading will be dealt with later.

THE SPOT MONTH

Unlike securities of a listed company (which are supposed to exist in perpetuity unless the firm goes belly-up) futures contracts have a termination month at which time they are relegated to the history books. The last month (contract expiration month) in which a contract can trade is referred to as the "spot" month.

While it is premature to discuss spread trading tactics as applied to the spot month, I want to convey one simple, important spread trading rule. I do not keep any spread position(s) open after the last day of the month preceding the spot month...ever! Close all spreads on or before the last business day of the month preceding the spot month. For example, the December S&P's spot month is sometime in November. Hence, if you are trading the S&P spread, exit the position on or before the last trading day in October.

While it is true that holding a spread trade open going into the spot month may result in larger profits, it is also true that you can be hit with a "notice of delivery" (commonly called a warehouse receipt) on the long side of the spread and a "demand" to deliver on the short side. My advice is don't wait for either notice. While it is true that you can immediately offset the spread, it just isn't worth the hassle. You may also have to pay one day's storage charge, to boot.

TAX TREATMENT ON SPREADS

Consult with your CPA or tax attorney.

SPREAD PROFITS

Trading spreads can be very lucrative. A number of spreads, when timed correctly, have rewarded traders with thousands of dollars in profits per spread with far less risk than if a trader took only "net" positions. If your timing is correct, you can generate additional thousands of dollars in profits by reversing the position. Three spreads with a high profit potential are: (1) the wheat/corn, (2) the July vs. Nov. soybean spread, and (3) the pork belly/hog spreads.

SPREAD MARGINS

Spread margins are about 40% under the "original margin" requirements for trading "net" positions. As a matter of fact, intra-commodity spreads have no minimum margin requirements. These spreads can be "marked-to-market." This means that as long as there is equity in the account, the trader is home free. However, margin requirements are subject to change by the exchange itself, or by your brokerage company, or by both. Usually there is a margin requirement set by the firm you are trading through. The margin is designed to protect the firm. Check with your A. E. for margin rules. They do change.

SPREADS AND MORE SPREADS

As of this writing, there are over forty-five different commodities listed for trading with seemingly a new commodity being listed every month or thereabouts. Each one has between six and nine trading months extending out about two years. The spread trader, therefore, has literally several hundred trading combinations to choose from.

To know that there exists potentially hundreds of trades is one thing; knowing about each one is something else again. The method I use is simple and neat. I have a 4"x6" file box containing two sets of cards. One set has each of the twelve months printed on a card. The other set has lined cards on which I list the different spreads and the months in which they are expected to make a top or bottom. If a spread, based on historical reference, makes more than one top or bottom during the year, I write the spread down on each of the appropriate "month" cards. Each month I check the file on which spreads are expected to make a high or low. If I am doing a twin line on any of them, I make a note to that effect on the twin-line spread graph. If I am not presently doing a twin-line graph, one will be made up going back 30 to 40 days.

CONTRA SEASONAL SPREAD ACTION

As mentioned earlier, spreads have a tendency to conform in seasonal fashion. Many will consistently make highs and lows at certain times of the year. Sometimes, however, they don't. If they are due to head lower and then continue higher, or the reverse, they are said to be moving contra-seasonally.

A contra-seasonal action offers the astute trader an opportunity to possibly profit in handsome fashion. A contra-seasonal move is rarely fleeting and generally lasts for quite awhile. The first twin line signal in line with the prevailing direction of the spread should be heeded and a position put on as soon as possible (this point will become clearer in forthcoming chapters describing the application of the twin-line method).

SPREAD PORTFOLIO OPPORTUNITIES

A portfolio of spreads can be structured so as to take advantage of twin-line bull and bear spread signals. Additionally, these same spreads can be found in a number of commodity families which allows for solid diversification, a main-spring to generating solid profits in an account. A later chapter has been devoted to this subject. For now, just realize that you are capable of executing any type of strategy with spreads.

SPREAD LOSSES

I would not be completely candid if I neglected to mention that some spread trades will be losers. Where there is a chance to profit, there is a risk involved. If you put on a spread the wrong way, you will most likely lose money. Losses may also result from using the wrong type of order, and not employing stop protection. More on spread orders and stops in subsequent chapters.

Chapter 2

Spread Trading Orders

The first thing to learn about a spread order is that it is composed of two sets of instructions. One part of the order is to go long a contract(s), and the second part is to go short a contract(s), or vice-versa. Since there are two sides to a spread, there must be two orders—one for each side.

Spread position instructions do not have to be entered simultaneously on the same order although usually they are. The reason why this is so will be explained later in this chapter, but for now just accept the fact that different order procedures exist in putting on or offsetting spread positions.

A SPREAD MARKET ORDER

A market order is one in which a position(s) will be put on or closed out at the market (the best available price). The market order is the simplest to execute.

The spread market order should be used when putting on or closing out grain spreads (whose contracts are listed on the Chicago Board of Trade) with one exception: Do not use a CBT market order where one or both sides of the spread involves an oats contract.

A market order should be employed whenever a mental stop has been hit or penetrated, regardless of the contracts forming the spread or the particular exchange in question. Stop protection will be thoroughly explained in another chapter. What you need to be aware of at this juncture is that a stop order is designed to get you out of an untenable position. Don't play games with stop orders...ever!

A market order can also be used when opening or offsetting a spread in the financial and stock index markets. These markets are highly liquid and the price you receive will be the same or close to the price of the last trade. One exception to using a market order in the stock index contracts is when one or both sides of the spread involve the Value-Line index. Avoid using market orders in this case.

The meat complex, coffee, cocoa, sugar, cotton, orange juice, lumber and plywood contracts really are not suitable for the use of market orders. However, keep in mind the proviso mentioned earlier if your stop price is hit and you must quickly exit the trade. If your mental stop is hit or penetrated do not hesitate to use a market order.

At this time a word of caution is in order; the "true" price of a futures contract may be far removed from the last price shown on the monitor. You see, all too often, especially in thinly traded contracts, the price on the monitor may be 20, 30 or more points away from the "true" price. It does not reflect the bid and asked price. Contracts listed on New York, Kansas City, and the Mid-America exchanges are notorious for bid and ask prices being some distance removed from the last recorded price at which a trade was effected. Cotton is one shining example of what I am talking about. The asking price might be anywhere from 20 to 40 points, or more, from the last trading price. And, with a one point move in cotton equal to five dollars, you are looking at a move against you of between one hundred and two hundred dollars. A large disadvantage, to be sure. There are two approaches to this problem which we will now look at.

THE SPREAD PRICE ORDER

A spread price order is one in which the spread difference is part of the order. If you get your price, you are in the spread position.

An "or better" price is a price less than the one stipulated on the order. If you go short, expecting lower prices, and you use a price order, the "or better" price must be higher than the stipulated price on the order. While this does happen quite often in net position trading, it is rare that a spread trader will get a better spread difference than the one on the price order.

One situation you will experience frequently is when you see the spread difference hit your price or even go below or above it, as the case may be, and at the end of the day have your broker tell you that the order was not executed. Floor brokers are under exchange rules which stipulate they must fill a net position order if the price trades below the price on the order (if the trader wants to go long) or above the price (if it is an order to go short). This rule doesn't apply to spreads because different months or contracts are involved. So if you get back an "ND" (nothing done), don't fret. It happens very often.

SEPARATE TRADING ORDERS

This is the second method used when spreading in a thin or slow trading market. You place two orders, one to go long, the second to go short. Either order can be a market or price order. Not all trading months are thin or slow. The near month is usually quite active so a market or price order close to the last trading price will generally be executed.

In the previous paragraph I used the words "usually" and "generally." Let me back up a little so that you will know why I carefully chose them. Suppose you put in a price order for one leg of the spread fully expecting it to be filled, at the same time you put in a second order to complete the spread. At the end of the day you find out only one of the two orders were filled. You are now "net" long or short a position instead of having a spread. That is why it is imperative that you find out if both sides of the spread were filled before the end of trading.

You may be wondering if it is at all possible for a spread contract to trade at a better price and still have the order come back as not having been executed. Well, yes. A better spread price than your order does not guarantee a fill. In a fast market where there may be many buy and sell orders at a certain price, the broker may not be able to fill all of them before the price moves away.

LEGGING INTO A SPREAD

While similar in results to writing two spread orders, legging into or out

25

of a spread is done for a different reason. Legging in or out is done in order to (a) obtain better prices, or (b) to protect a profitable trade (never a losing trade). Legging in is somewhat more sophisticated and should only be undertaken after you have gained considerable spread experience.

I mentioned a situation just now which does need some clarification. Traders have the mistaken notion that they can protect a loss on a net position by putting on an equal and opposite number of positions. What they have done is to "lock in" their loss. This all too frequently just exacerbates the problem. The losses increased because the spread did not act in the way they hoped it would. If you ever trade net positions, and they move against you, get out of the trade. Never spread a losing position.

THE SPREAD QUOTE

Just as you can obtain a "floor" quote for a net position, you can also get one for a spread. All the broker has to do is call the exchange floor. If you want a floor quote ask him to find out. Then, if it is to your liking, ask him to get a confirmation of the trade from the floor at that spread difference. Some brokers are loathe to take the time to call the floor of the exchange. If your broker hems and haws, take your business elsewhere.

Chapter 3

You And Your Broker

In the main, this chapter is about your broker and what you can do to protect yourself from certain unscrupulous practices which are perpetrated by commodity brokers against the trading public every day. I speak as one who knows, for I was a commodity broker and will be one again after this book is finished. I have no axes to grind. This is not a vendetta. My only motivation is a responsibility I feel to alert my readers to the realities of what they're up against.

The first "no-no" is never, and I mean never, give an account executive discretionary trading authority over your account. To do so is to play Russian Roulette with a bullet in "all" the chambers.

Why am I so dead set against giving trading authority to an account executive? AE's work on a commission. If they don't trade your account, they don't earn a living. I am sure you have met many sorry traders who were foolish (and poorer) because they handed over trading authority to AE's. I can almost guarantee that you will lose money if you let your AE trade your account. I strongly recommend you make an all out effort to "call your own shots" and make your own trading decisions.

While it is not advisable to give your broker trading authority, it is worse still when the broker trades your account without your written permission. You may be surprised to learn that many brokers do just that. Recourse against the AE is difficult because it is your word against the AE's. How can you prove he executed an order without your permission?

An unauthorized execution is wrong...period. And if you let one unauthorized trade slip by, you are just begging to lose your money.

RECORD ALL CONVERSATIONS

I cannot state too strongly this sound advice. To protect yourself, your equity, your peace of mind, you must record all conversations with your account executive. Did you know that the exchanges record all conversations coming into the floor? The price of a recorder and telephone induction pick-up costs less than thirty dollars. A small price to pay for protection and a wise investment indeed.

Do you legally have to inform your AE that all conversations will be recorded? I would, to be on the safe side. If he protests, well, I'll address that point later. First things first. When you open an account you will have to sign some forms. The first is a customer account form. You will sign it in two places and sometimes in a third section. Whenever you sign your name, insert these words as close to your signature(s) as you can, "all conversations are recorded. No audio (beep) signal is used and no verbal acknowledgment is given," then initial the written message. Make sure this information appears on the duplicate or photocopy of the account form which *must* be returned to you.

There is a section on the customer account form which, if included, should be crossed out. It is the "arbitration clause." This clause states that you agree to settle disputes through arbitration. It may include a sentence which states that you are giving up your right to sue the broker and/or his firm in court. That clause has been declared illegal by the SEC. While the SEC does not have jurisdiction over commodity brokers, their edict should be, and I believe is supported by the CFTC (Commodity Futures Trading Commission). The CFTC does have jurisdiction over commodity brokers. Regardless, you are not obligated to sign the arbitration clause, so don't.

The second form is called a "risk disclosure" statement. It purportedly warns you of the risk involved in futures trading. Unfortunately, it does not warn you about, nor explain your avenues of redress, against brokers and their firms.

All right, you have given notice that all conversations will be recorded, what is your next move? Before you dial your broker for the first time, insert a tape into your unit and record the date and time. With the unit still recording, dial the broker's number. Whatever you do, don't stop the recording. If for instance the phone is answered by a switchboard operator, keep recording. When the AE gets on the line tell him that this call, and all future calls, will be recorded. After you conclude the conversation indicate the time so that the call rests between a starting and concluding time frame. That tape should not be used to record other conversations because it contains your verbal acknowledgment that henceforth all conversations will be recorded without notice of that fact.

If your broker is not delighted when you tell him you will be recording all conversations, simply inform him that you are doing so to protect him and you against possible errors cropping up in the account. If he protests, file a complaint (you do not need an attorney) with either the CFTC or the National Futures Association (NFA) or both. Both main offices are in Washington, D. C. and they also have regional offices. Then find another AE.

Recording conversations after the initial contact has been made requires little preparation. First record the date and time, then record the second time to encapsulate the conversation between two time frames. By the way, make sure the few inches of leader tape which cannot be used to record anything have passed. Judging by the time I've spent on this topic and the detail with which I have outlined this safety measure, it should be readily apparent that recording conversations is something I feel strongly about. It will give you much needed proof should events turn against you, and could save you a substantial amount of money.

PROTECTION FROM DISCOUNTERS

Use of a discount broker is a smart move as you will save upwards of 50% to 70% in commission costs. However, do not use any discount futures brokerage firm which is not a member of at least one American Commodity Exchange. It does not matter how well they claim to be capitalized, their business affiliation, etc. If the company goes "belly up," the only recourse you have is to file a claim with the bankruptcy court. If they go out of business for any reason, you don't stand a prayer of ever seeing any of your funds again. Not so if the company is an Exchange

29

member. You do have protection under Exchange rules. The moral!—If a discount firm (and there are a few) is not a member of at least one American Commodity Exchange (preferably two or three), don't trade through that company. Incidentally, a discount futures firm does not have to be an Exchange member firm to accept accounts. The Exchange requires only that orders be executed through a member firm. That procedure does not protect your funds.

SHOULD A CTA MANAGE YOUR ACCOUNT?

Definitely not! There are no commodity trading advisors exclusively engaged in trading spreads, to my knowledge, and none of them use the twin-line method of spread analysis. There are a number of other reasons CTAs turn me off. CTAs look for the quick, fast buck which is why they basically trade options and net positions.

A CTA is registered as such with the government. As long as he did not steal the gold fillings from his mother's mouth, he will get his ticket. Educational requirements do not exist, nor is one required to take a test based on knowledge of the commodity futures markets to become registered. That fact should tell you something about the caliber of some CTAs. In addition there are numerous financial costs to you which are paid to the CTA whether or not your account shows a profit.

The usual procedure is for a CTA to trade your account under a "Power of Attorney." In addition, you sign a partial release which allows the broker used by the CTA to pay him his fees out of your account. For handling your money, the CTA receives three fees. The first is a management fee. Each month a predetermined percent of the total equity in the account is withdrawn and paid to the CTA. The second cost against your account is an administrative fee which is tacked on. And the third and last charge is a percent of net profits (net profits being those profits after accrued losses have been deducted). This fee is on the order of 15% to 20%. The CTA makes money whether you win or lose. These charges are all legal as long as they are made known to you in writing, and they are. When you combine the uncertainty in finding a reliable CTA with the big financial bite they get out of you in good times and bad, a strong case is made to avoid CTAs and, again, to take charge of your own trading.

SPREAD LETTER SERVICES

While not directly related to the material in this chapter, I want to cover this point before we begin studying the nitty-gritty of our subject. The following spread service is the only one I know of worth looking into.

Write to:

Spread Scope, Inc.
Post Office Box 5841
Mission Hills, CA 91345

Chapter 4

Understanding Spread Values

Before I begin an in-depth look at my twin-line spread methodology, it's important that you're comfortable working with spread values. It's not complicated but essential for you to understand. Let's start with the grain complex which is composed of corn, wheat, oats, soybeans, soybean meal and soybean oil.

Grains are traded in dollars, cents and fractions of a cent. The value of a one cent move in the grain complex is equal to fifty ($50.00) dollars. A ¼ cent move is equal to $12.50, a ½ cent equals $25.00, and ¾ equals $37.50.

Grain prices (excluding soybean meal and soybean oil) are written with a fraction or its numerical equivalent: 3.06 ¼ or 3.0625 have the same value as three dollars six and a quarter cents. We convert the fractions to their numerical equivalents when finding spread differences; 4.15 ¾ becomes 4.1575, and 375 ½ is 3.7550 or three dollars seventy-five and a half cents.

If you are back-tracking a grain using Videcom equipment by Comtrend, a new wrinkle needs to be understood. Instead of showing a fraction or its equivalent value, you will see something like this: 306-2, 308-4 or 301-6. The 2, 4 and 6 mean ¼, ½ or ¾ of a cent. I suppose it is easier for the computer bank to store these numbers rather than fractions. If you see 306 ¼, 3.0625 or 306-2, they all mean three dollars, six and a quarter cents.

Bean and oil prices do not use fractions. Price movements are expressed in points (as are all commodities except the four grains and the MMI). What distinguishes points in one contract from another contract is the dollar value per point. In meal it is $10.00 a point, oil is $6.00, etc.

When putting on a number of spreads in which each of the contracts has a different point value, you use the total value of each contract. You find the money difference and plot it on the twin line graph. A money scale for each is written in on the left side of the graph paper. The reasons for using a money value difference compared to a point difference will soon become clear.

To set up a soybean meal vs. soybean oil spread you perform one simple change in the location of the decimal point in meal, and a quick multiplication yields the money value for an oil contract. Meal's contract size is 100 tons. A posted price for meal looks like this: 171.50 or one hundred and seventy one dollars and fifty cents per ton. This works out to 17,150 for 100 tons. Move the decimal point over one place to the left and you have the total price for one full contract. Do this on the high, low and closing meal contract prices.

Oil trades in cents per pound (20.45 is equal to twenty cents and forty five points). One point is equal to $6.00. A soybean oil contract contains 60,000 pounds of oil. Since we are going to multiply contract size by cents per pound, move the decimal point all the way to the left so that 20.45 becomes .2045. Multiplying both numbers gives you a total oil contract value of 12,270. Subtracting this total from the total meal contract value gives you a plus (+) value of $4,880.00, the spread money difference between meal and oil.

In doing the platinum/gold spread, you don't double the dollar value of platinum because its contract size is 50 oz. and gold's contract size is 100. What you do instead is to put on a 2 to 1 spread. Two platinum versus one gold. The spread difference is found by subtracting one value from the other, using the value for one platinum contract. In effect, you want to do the same amount of ounces Platinum vis-a-vis Gold.

In the corn/oats spread, you generally use the value of two oat contracts vs. the value of one corn contract. Even though both contracts individually are the same size (5,000 bushels) and price values are computed in the same way, there is a major difference between the two grains. When converted into animal feed, the milling of two bushels of oats for feed only slightly exceeds that for corn. While some spreaders do use one oat vs. one corn, it is not really correct due to the corn/oats ratio (i. e.—the difference in the amount of feed when milled).

Simple subtraction and multiplication is all that is required to find any spread difference, with just one exception. The one exception being any contract whose value is computed in 32nds of a point (i.e.—bonds and GNMA futures contracts move in basis points with each point equal to 1/32nd). To subtract one such contract from the other requires a simple modification to our usual method of subtraction.

Let's say that a T-Bond price is 71.05, and the GNMA price is 69.06 and you want to find the spread difference. Reduce the T-Bond price of 71.05 and make it 70.37. What did you do? You simply converted the 71 5/32 to 70 and 37/32, or 70.37. Notice the decimal point; numbers to its left are full percentage values and those to the right are basis points or 32nds. The .37 is now higher than the .06 in the GNMA price of 69.06 to simplify subtraction. Subtract and you will get 1.31 or one basis point less than a full 2 units difference (units being % of 100).

Let's do one more 32nd spread. We change the T-Bond to 70.06 and the GNMA to 69.05. Since the .06 is larger we can just subtract and we get a change of .01 or 31 basis points less than 2%. It is the numbers to the right of the decimal point which tells you which kind of subtraction to use.

Chapter 5

Spread Work Form Data

The first of the two parts of my spread trading twin-line methodology is the spread work form. While not complex in its construction, it is, nevertheless, a little involved. I decided to present the knowledge required to achieve a thorough understanding of the work form in three separate chapters. Chapter 5 and 6 will teach you what goes into the work form and how to use the data. Chapter 11 is devoted to sharpening your "feeling" about spreads through viewing the work form subjectively.

Curiosity is good if one does not draw a negative conclusion from a "look-see" examination of data. If you are like me, the first thing you did was to browse through this study, reading a paragraph here and there, before settling down to a serious perusal of its contents. You may have opened this book to the chapter devoted to the many twin-line spread graphs and noticed that each contained high/low spread differential lines. Opting for a quick look-see as to how I knew what values to graph, you may have turned to the chapters on the spread work form and, quite possibly, felt a pang of apprehension. It would be natural to wonder how it is possible to obtain two numerical spread values when, at the top of each form, there are three columns denoting the high, low and last spread difference. For now, suffice it to say that I use two of the three spread differences. Much more on that topic in due course.

To understand the three columns used on the spread form, it is suggested you open your newspaper to the commodity section.

A number of columnar headings will greet you on the Futures stat page: open, high, low, close, change and open interest (OI). In our work, we are only concerned with the high, low and last price. The opening price is not used, nor are we interested in the daily price change. Open interest has relevance for us insofar as liquidity is a factor. More on liquidity, shortly.

One price column deserves special mention because it may become confusing. The "last" price may or may not be the final or settlement price. The confusion may arise when the last price is different in the final edition of the newspaper from the early edition.

At the final bell, denoting the close of trading for that day on the floor of the exchange, trading often becomes hectic. The floor brokers may not be able to match up the many buy and sell orders. Add to that the possibility of price errors which may result due to faulty transmission of last minute orders, incorrect recording of same, misplaced orders, etc. It then becomes obvious why many minutes may elapse (sometimes hours) before the settlement price is known.

If you have a monitor at home or call your AE for the last price, he'll glance at his monitor and relay the information. The last price on the monitor may not be the settlement price for the same reasons enumerated.

Newspapers who operate under a deadline may use the last price on the monitor for their next edition. This may not be the settlement price. It pays to wait a couple of hours after the markets are officially closed before using your monitor or to call the AE for price quotes. The monitor will update and eventually show the settlement price for the day's trading.

The final price is a misnomer. It can mean the last recorded price or the settlement price, depending on what the inquirer has in mind. Ask for the settlement price, or if you are taking the data out of your paper, wait for the evening edition. It contains the settlement price under the column headed "last" price. I use the word "last" on the work form because there is not enough room to write in the word settlement. However, it is the settlement price that is used when I update my graphs.

Although I discussed liquidity earlier, I believe it is so important to the spreader it deserves mention again. Do not attempt to spread a contract month in which the open interest is less than 3500 contracts. Especially, if you are going to use a market order. In a thin market (one in which the open interest is small) you will get killed on the spread price. Watch open interest before putting on a spread.

The spread work form contains the highest, lowest and last prices of the two contracts, which were reached during the market day. From the three sets of prices for each contract, we obtain the highest spread difference and the lowest spread difference. The two differences represent the spread's range for that day. They are then graphed onto the twin-line spread form.

The high price columns may or may not represent the highest spread difference. The low columns may or may not represent the lowest spread difference. The last price column may represent either the highest spread difference, the lowest spread difference, or some "medium range" spread difference (if it's a medium spread difference, it is disregarded). Please reread and memorize this paragraph.

The difference between one contract's high price and the second contract's high price may be less than the difference between the two contracts' low prices. The reason is because both of the high prices may be so close together the spread difference may be quite narrow. The lows of the two contracts may be much wider; hence, the settlement price could be wider or narrower than either of the other two price differences.

Remember what I have said, but don't think about it at this time or you will become confused. For now, accept what I say. The confusion sets in when you mentally compare plus and minus spread differentials. You are always looking for the highest spread difference and the lowest difference from the three sets of prices. It doesn't matter from which column you get your high or low differential, and it doesn't matter if one gives a minus reading and another a positive spread difference. The procedure is still the same.

The column headings lose their meaning as far as the spread differences are concerned. Once you obtain the three differentials you find which one of them is the highest and which is the lowest. In other words we are dealing with two factors. The first is to get the spread differential from the high, low and last price of the contracts. The second is to concentrate only on the spread differences, locating the highest and the lowest differential from the three price levels. I realize I am being redundant but I want you to fix firmly in your mind what I am saying. One set of prices can result in a high or a low spread difference. In theory, you may have trouble visualizing this concept particularly as it applies to a minus difference. So let's clear the air on that point.

Is it possible to subtract a higher number from a lower number (never mind which price column you are using)? Of course, it is. The only change is the sign, plus or minus, which precedes the result.

Suppose you are doing a spread on wheat vs. corn. In the three columns you have wheat first and corn second. Today's high price for wheat is $350.00 and the high for corn is $349.00. What is the spread difference, and is it a plus or minus change? Since the spread is wheat's price versus corn's price (and since from the prices shown, wheat is the higher of the two), you know that the sign is a plus (wheat over corn). The difference is a + .01¢.

In time, the wheat's price may fall below that of corn. The spread is still a wheat vs. corn spread. So what sign precedes the spread (price) difference when wheat goes under corn? Let's see. Today's price of wheat is $3.07, and the price of corn is $3.08. What is the difference (and why) and what sign is used?

Since we are dealing with the price of wheat versus the price of corn, when wheat's price goes under the price of corn we have a − .01¢ favoring corn. To put it another way, the price of corn is higher than the price of wheat (remember it's wheat vs. corn).

Does it matter in which of the three price columns the spreads negative change has taken place? Absolutely not. We now are only interested in the three spread differences irrespective of which price column they are derived from.

To graph a minus spread difference on a twin line graph when the preceding differentials have all been plus differences, you must split the graph in half by drawing a line across the middle denoting the top half as the plus section and the lower half as the minus sections. All positive differences are recorded above the line and all minus differences recorded below the line. The middle line has no price value because it simply separates or divides the page in half; hence, we refer to that line as the zero (0) line.

While it is true that not all spread graphs contain a zero line because some spreads do not turn minus, this fact creates a small problem. How should you scale a twin-line graph preparatory to posting high and low differences. Should you include a zero line? I will address that question in another section.

How do you find spread differences on the work form when you are doing two oats vs. one corn? You double the high, low and last price for one contract of oats (posting the totals in their respective columns). Then take the price of one contract of corn and place it in its appropriate column. You simply subtract the corn from the oat's price. Spread work forms depicting the different types of spreads will be found in the next chapter.

Chapter 6

Different Spread Work Forms

It would be a wise idea to cut out and retain the commodity price data page from your newspaper on a daily basis even if you have access to a data bank or Videcom (Comtrend) Data Bases. Should you become interested in doing a particular spread, you will have the price data at your fingertips for bringing the graph up to date. It would also be a smart move, when doing a spread work form, to use a pencil for posting the data. Errors do occur.

Just by eyeballing the many types of work forms on the following pages, you will have no problem in duplicating their construction. You have nine sections, so divide the sheet into nine parts.

The top of the spread work form contains information about the spread. I sometimes write the starting date on the sheet. To the far right on the top line, I insert the page number if I am going to save the sheets. The page number will keep the data in numerical order.

On the following pages are exact reproductions of actual worksheets I've used. I've had them included "as is" because this is the form in which you will be using and applying them. Here neatness doesn't count; accuracy does. There is rhyme and reason as to why I've included these particular work forms in the particular order they're in. Each of these work forms was used in the creation of one of the graphs presented in Chapter 9. The work forms are presented here in the same order as the corresponding spread analyses (and graphs) are presented later in the text. You will be referring back to these work forms once Chapter 9 is reached.

JULY 84 CORN VS JULY 84 OATS

MONTH DATE	CORN HIGH	OATS HIGH	DIFF HIGH	CORN LOW	OATS LOW	DIFF LOW	CORN CLOSE	OATS CLOSE	DIFF CLOSE
1-26	33425	18075	15350	33050	17650	15400	33175	17925	15250
27	33700	18000	157.00	33175	17825	15350	33225	17875	153.50
30	332.75	17925	153.50	330.00	176.50	153.50	331.75	177.75	15400
31	333.75	178.25	15525	331.25	177.25	154.00	332.50	177.50	155.00
2-1	33400	17800	15600	33175	175.75	15600	33375	17750	15625
2	33750	178.75	158.75	33500	176.75	158.25	335.50	176.75	158.75
3	33500	17500	160.00	33350	17350	160.00	33500	174.75	160.25
6	33525	174.50	160.75	33200	17200	160.00	33475	173.50	161.25
7	334.75	175.00	159.75	333.25	173.00	160.25	33375	173.00	160.75
8	334.50	17400	160.50	332.75	172.75	16000	333.50	17350	160.00
9	33325	174.25	15900	33050	170.00	16050	332.00	17025	16175
10	331.50	170.25	161.25	329.50	167.75	161.75	329.50	167.75	161.75
13	328.25	168.25	160.00	324.00	166.25	15775	326.25	167.00	159.25
14	32700	16850	158.50	32275	16650	156.25	32325	16700	15625
15	326.25	170.50	155.75	32325	168.00	15525	325.00	169.50	155.50
16	326.25	170.75	155.50	323.75	168.25	15550	324.25	17075	153.50
17	32500	17250	15250	322.00	170.50	151.50	323.00	171.25	151.75
21	322.50	170.50	152.00	320.25	168.00	15225	321.75	169.25	152.50
22	328.25	17100	157.25	323.00	169.75	153.25	326.75	170.50	156.25
23	328.25	17100	157.25	324.75	167.75	15700	326.25	168.75	157.50
24	327.75	170.00	157.75	325.50	16900	156.50	326.50	16900	157.50
27	327.25	17000	157.25	324.50	16800	156.50	327.00	16950	15750
28	32950	170.75	158.75	32500	168.50	156.50	326.25	168.75	15750
29	33250	173.50	15900	326.25	169.00	157.25	331.50	171.50	160.00
3-1	33375	173.50	160.25	33100	171.50	159.50	33225	173.00	159.25
2	335.50	17550	160.00	33400	174.25	159.75	335.00	175.00	160.00
5	33700	17700	16000	33425	17525	15900	336.75	17675	16000
6	33975	17700	16275	33650	17575	16075	33875	17650	162.25
7	33850	17550	16300	33600	17450	16150	33825	17525	16300
8	33825	17775	16050	33600	17400	16200	33800	17750	16050
9	343.25	17825	165.00	33875	17700	16175	34150	17775	16375
12	34250	17750	16500	339.50	17600	16350	34050	17650	164.00
13	34300	17675	16625	34100	17600	16500	34125	17650	16475
14	34400	17700	16700	34075	17550	16525	34375	17600	16775
15	34600	17925	16675	34275	17675	16600	34600	17850	16750
16	34650	17875	16775	34425	17650	16775	34500	17650	168.50
19	34475	17600	16875	34300	17450	16850	34475	17525	16950
20	34750	17575	17175	34225	17300	16925	34725	17575	171.50
21	34975	17900	17075	34600	17525	17075	34825	17700	17125
22	35000	17950	17050	34700	17650	17050	34925	17750	17175

JULY 84 VS DEC 84 COTTON

JULY HIGH	DEC HIGH	DEC HIGH	JULY LOW	DEC LOW	DIFF LOW	JULY LAST	DEC LAST	DIFF LAST
7600	7135	+465	7560	7105	+455	7585	7125	+460
7670	7150	+520	7580	7115	+465	7633	7139	+494
7650	7164	+486	7601	7139	+462	7602	7141	+461
7689	7195	+494	7620	7135	+485	7654	7171	+483
7701	7205	+496	7660	7161	+499	7665	7175	+494
7695	7205	+490	7660	7165	+495	7664	7172	+492
7680	7195	+485	7620	7150	+470	7642	7150	+492
7635	7191	+444	7590	7161	+429	7625	7187	+438
7650	7205	+445	7601	7165	+436	7650	7202	+448
7669	7224	+445	7605	7191	+414	7610	7205	+405
7610	7215	+395	7480	7165	+315	7487	7180	+307
7520	7180	+340	7451	7135	+316	7460	7150	+310
7445	7145	+300	7401	7120	+281	7405	7143	+262
7505	7175	+330	7422	7120	+302	7446	7152	+294
7514	7180	+334	7446	7141	+305	7452	7146	+306
7500	7165	+335	7453	7140	+313	7495	7162	+333
7695	7359	+336	7610	7280	+330	7695	7352	+343
7675	7358	+317	7615	7283	+332	7670	7345	+325
7785	7400	+385	7660	7325	+335	7700	7327	+373
7775	7340	+435	7695	7285	+410	7761	7302	+459
7830	7340	+490	7760	7282	+478	7827	7327	+500
7887	7364	+523	7790	7305	+485	7864	7342	+522
7850	7347	+503	7800	7315	+485	7836	7342	+494
7860	7370	+490	7820	7335	+485	7847	7363	+484
7880	7389	+491	7815	7340	+475	7874	7385	+489
7970	7465	+505	7895	7400	+495	7967	7462	+505
7990	7485	+505	7932	7437	+495	7943	7443	+500
7943	7448	+495	7880	7420	+460	7887	7422	+465
7895	7415	+480	7840	7402	+438	7892	7411	+481
7990	7465	+525	7860	7406	+454	7967	7442	+525
8050	7485	+565	7985	7450	+535	8047	7485	+562
8145	7500	+645	8020	7465	+555	8130	7490	+640
8135	7500	+635	8065	7462	+603	8097	7471	+626
8110	7490	+620	8062	7455	+607	8107	7487	+620
8115	7496	+619	8083	7466	+617	8095	7477	+618
8095	7490	+605	8020	7450	+570	8062	7472	+590
8075	7480	+595	8006	7460	+546	8055	7480	+575
8125	7540	+585	8015	7470	+545	8111	7532	+579
8185	7585	+600	8090	7525	+565	8180	7573	+607
8185	7569	+616	8137	7520	+617	8160	7522	+638

NOV 84 VS MAR 84 ORANGE JUICE

NOV HIGH	MAR HIGH	DIFF HIGH	NOV LOW	MAR LOW	DIFF LOW	NOV CLOSE	MAR CLOSE	DIFF CLOSE
179.50	176.25	+325	178.00	17560	+240	179.00	17560	+340
17985	17700	+285	17890	17580	+310	17930	17675	+255
17950	17675	+275	17820	17605	+215	17850	17605	+245
17910	17670	+240	17785	17600	+185	17910	17670	+240
17950	17675	+275	17765	17605	+160	17825	17605	+220
17775	17575	+200	17715	17530	+185	17715	17540	+175
18030	17800	+230	17725	17575	+150	18000	17800	+200
18125	17900	+225	17910	17750	+160	18090	17825	+265
18435	18200	+235	18160	17825	+335	18435	18200	+235
18565	18270	+295	18380	18120	+260	18480	18240	+240
18500	18270	+230	18350	18150	+250	18380	18160	+220
18380	18150	+230	18300	18070	+230	18320	18070	+250
18300	18040	+260	17820	17580	+240	17820	17630	+190
17825	17750	+75	17620	17650	-30	17750	17710	+40
17770	17750	+20	17675	17675	00	17740	17710	+30
17975	17900	+75	17730	17710	+20	17950	17900	+50
18150	18090	+60	17960	17940	+20	18025	17980	+45
18020	17950	+70	17880	17900	-20	17930	17935	-5
17985	17990	-5	17930	17925	+5	17975	17940	+35
180.10	17990	+20	179.10	17925	-15	18000	17990	+10
17990	18000	-10	179.15	17910	+5	179.15	179.10	+5
17895	17900	-5	17710	17850	-140	17850	17875	-25
18030	17980	+50	17965	17950	+15	17975	17950	+25
18050	17980	+70	17950	17950	00	18000	17965	+35

(Mar 12/April 17-84)   **SEP 84 VS MAR 85 EURODOLLAR**

SEP HIGH	MAR HIGH	DIFF HIGH	SEP LOW	MAR LOW	DIFF LOW	SEP CLOSE	MAR CLOSE	DIFF CLOSE
88.63	88.05	+ 58	88.53	88.00	+ 53	88.61	88.05	+56
88.65	88.05	+ 60	88.58	88.00	+58	88.61	88.05	+56
88.69	88.10	+ 59	88.61	88.06	+ 55	88.62	88.06	+56
88.60	88.01	+59	88.51	87.96	+55	88.54	87.98	+56
88.55	88.00	+ 55	88.50	87.94	+56	88.55	88.00	+55
88.67	88.09	+ 58	88.49	87.95	+54	88.49	87.95	+54
88.46	87.89	+ 57	88.37	87.81	+56	88.38	87.81	+57
88.38	87.79	+ 59	88.20	87.60	+ 60	88.26	87.66	+60
88.30	87.70	+ 60	88.26	87.67	+59	88.27	87.67	+60
88.26	87.66	+ 60	88.17	87.54	+ 63	88.23	87.64	+ 59
88.30	87.69	+ 61	88.23	87.63	+ 60	88.23	87.63	+ 60
88.33	87.72	+ 61	88.30	87.70	+ 60	88.32	87.71	+ 61
88.43	87.81	+ 62	88.31	87.71	+ 60	88.31	87.71	+ 60
88.39	87.74	+ 65	88.32	87.71	+ 61	88.37	87.73	+ 64
88.44	87.74	+ 70	88.34	87.69	+ 65	88.35	87.70	+ 65
88.32	87.65	+ 67	88.15	87.58	+ 67	88.25	87.59	+ 66
88.36	87.67	+ 69	88.22	87.53	+ 69	88.23	87.54	+ 69
88.21	87.49	+ 72	88.06	87.33	+ 73	88.11	87.38	+ 73
88.12	87.40	+ 72	88.06	87.35	+ 71	88.09	87.38	+ 71
88.18	87.44	+ 74	88.02	87.30	+ 72	88.07	87.35	+ 72
88.25	87.45	+ 80	88.12	87.41	+ 71	88.23	87.45	+ 78
88.28	87.48	+ 80	88.21	87.42	+ 79	88.27	87.48	+ 79.
88.31	87.49	+ 82	88.26	87.45	+ 81	88.27	87.46	+ 81
88.30	87.50	+ 80	88.27	87.46	+ 81	88.29	87.49	+ 80
88.38	87.57	+ 79	88.27	87.53	+ 74	88.38	87.57	+ 81
88.44	87.59	+ 85	88.21	87.42	+ 79	88.21	87.42	+ 79
88.20	87.40	+ 8A	88.10	87.33	+ 77	88.15	87.36	+ 79
88.26	87.46	+ 80	88.18	87.40	+ 78	88.25	87.46	+ 79

MAR 84 BEANS VS JULY 84 BEANS

MAR HIGH	JULY HIGH	DIFF HIGH	MAR LOW	JULY LOW	DIFF LOW	MAR LAST	JULY LAST	DIFF LAST
70050	71900	-1850	68900	70800	-1900	69500	71300	-1800
70150	72050	-1900	69300	71300	-2000	69850	71725	-1875
69750	71700	-1950	68900	70950	-2050	69200	71000	-1800
69350	71200	-1850	68700	70650	-1950	68700	70650	-1950
71000	72800	-1800	69850	70900	-2050	70075	71900	-1825
71300	73150	-1850	70600	72500	-1900	70750	72650	-1900
72550	74500	-1550	71100	73150	-2050	72450	74350	-1900
75450	77350	-1900	73900	75900	-2000	75450	77350	-1900
78300	80200	-1900	74000	76000	-2000	75725	77500	-1750
77600	79300	-1700	76200	77900	-1700	76650	78150	-1500
76650	78100	-1450	73650	75150	-1500	76425	78000	-1575
77500	78900	-1400	73800	75400	-1600	74500	76200	-1700
75400	77000	-1600	74200	75800	-1600	75100	76500	-1400
77400	78800	-1400	76100	77600	-1500	76450	77700	-1250
76200	77600	-1400	74100	75800	-1700	75275	76650	-1375
78100	79200	-1100	74900	76400	-1500	78100	79200	-1100
80100	81000	-900	78800	80000	-1200	79325	80300	-975
81750	82300	-550	79100	80000	-900	81400	81900	-500
81950	82300	-350	80550	80500	+0050	81250	81000	+150
83800	83400	+400	80700	80600	+0100	83525	83075	+450
85000	84800	+200	81400	81500	-0100	82250	82300	-50
83200	83500	-300	82000	82000	0 0 0	82500	82800	-300
85500	85800	-300	83800	84100	-300	85500	85800	-300
88100	87800	+300	86000	86000	0 00	88000	87750	+250
90500	90500	0 00	87300	87500	-200	89650	88850	+800
92650	91850	+800	91000	90300	+700	92650	91850	+800
95650	94850	+800	90000	88850	+1150	94600	93550	+1050
95150	94300	+850	92150	91200	+950	93450	92400	+1050
91800	91000	+800	90450	89400	+1050	90450	89400	+1050

46

July 11, 83 **MAR 84 BEANS VS JULY 84 BEANS**

MAR HIGH	JULY HIGH	DIFF HIGH	MAR LOW	JULY LOW	DIFF LOW	MAR LAST	JULY LAST	DIFF LAST
89400	88400	+ 1000	87450	86400	+ 1050	87450	86400	+ 1050
90450	89400	+ 1050	90450	89400	+ 1050	90450	89400	+ 1050
93450	92400	+ 1050	92500	91200	+ 1300	93450	92400	+ 1050
95800	94400	+ 1400	93200	91900	+ 1300	95750	94100	+ 1650
98750	97100	+ 1650	94900	93800	+ 1100	96150	94725	+ 1425
96700	95600	+ 1100	93700	92750	+ 950	96550	95350	+ 1200
96475	95600	+ 875	93700	92800	+ 900	93900	92800	+ 1100
92400	91400	+ 1000	90900	89800	+ 1100	90900	89800	+ 1100
93400	92600	+ 800	90350	89600	+ 750	93150	92400	+ 750
93800	93250	+ 550	90150	89400	+ 750	90150	89400	+ 750
93150	92400	+ 750	90500	89700	+ 800	93150	92400	+ 750
95500	95100	+ 400	93300	93100	+ 200	95400	94850	+ 550
96400	96200	+ 200	94600	94500	+ 100	95500	95250	+ 250
95500	95600	- 100	94600	94500	+ 100	95300	95450	- 150
97650	97450	+ 200	96500	96300	+ 200	97150	96675	+ 475
97400	97000	+ 400	96300	96200	+ 100	96350	96250	+ 100
99350	99250	+ 100	93600	93600	0 00	93800	93650	+ 150
94300	93800	+ 500	91200	91200	0 00	91650	92000	- 350
92200	92500	- 300	88650	89000	- 350	88650	89000	- 350
90650	90700	- 50	86900	87500	- 600	90150	90450	- 300
93150	93450	- 300	90750	91300	- 550	93150	93450	- 300
94000	94100	- 100	91700	91900	- 200	92900	93050	- 150
95900	96050	- 50	95900	96050	- 150	95900	96050	- 150
98300	98200	+ 100	94800	95000	- 200	94900	95100	- 200
95600	95200	+ 400	92800	92400	+ 400	93500	92850	+ 650
93400	92800	+ 600	90500	89850	+ 650	90500	89850	+ 650
92100	91500	+ 600	89500	89000	+ 500	91900	91050	+ 850
93200	92200	+ 1000	88900	88050	+ 850	88900	88050	+ 850

47

MAR 84 PORK BELLIES VS JULY 84 PORK BELLIES

MAR HIGH	JULY HIGH	DIFF HIGH	MAR LOW	JULY LOW	DIFF LOW	MAR LAST	JULY LAST	DIFF LAST
5850	5750	+100	5670	5530	+140	5710	5550	+160
5710	5580	+130	5635	5500	+135	5690	5532	+158
5680	5562	+118	5650	5490	+160	5652	5500	+152
5700	5530	+170	5640	5515	+125	5660	5515	+145
5735	5595	+140	5680	5535	+145	5680	5562	+118
5785	5610	+175	5685	5610	+75	5780	5610	+170
5900	5750	+150	5840	5675	+165	5867	5712	+155
5885	5800	+85	5850	5695	+155	5880	5702	+178
5680	5560	+120	5680	5512	+168	5680	5512	+168
5825	5712	+113	5710	5610	+100	5755	5655	+100
5820	5680	+140	5665	5570	+95	5665	5570	+95
5670	5605	+65	5597	5555	+42	5657	5555	+102
5770	5665	+105	5505	5510	−5	5750	5662	+88
5770	5510	+260	5590	5470	+120	5595	5490	+105
5540	5480	+60	5445	5300	+145	5470	5317	+153
5610	5405	+205	5370	5350	+20	5607	5382	+225
5695	5525	+170	5530	5405	+125	5560	5420	+140
5620	5480	+140	5520	5420	+100	5610	5462	+148
5695	5550	+145	5550	5502	+48	5685	5525	+160
5760	5650	+110	5695	5580	+115	5755	5630	+125
5730	5650	+80	5590	5550	+40	5602	5552	+50
5635	5610	+25	5480	5510	−30	5560	5515	+45
5640	5565	+75	5540	5502	+38	5610	5517	+93
5640	5560	+80	5565	5502	+63	5590	5505	+85
5715	5605	+110	5590	5567	+23	5625	5575	+50
5665	5640	+25	5500	5570	−70	5540	5577	−37
5740	5777	−37	5510	5600	−90	5740	5777	−37
5940	5977	−37	5780	5860	−80	5915	5905	+10
6040	6105	−65	5855	5890	−35	6005	5990	+15

June 13, 83   **MAR 84 BELLIES VS JULY 84 BELLIES**

MAR HIGH	JULY HIGH	DIFF HIGH	MAR LOW	JULY LOW	DIFF LOW	MAR LAST	JULY LAST	DIFF LAST
6085	6080	+ 5	5872	5900	– 28	6072	6072	00
6125	6115	+10	6025	6002	+ 23	6062	6015	+47
6180	6115	+65	6020	5930	+ 90	6135	6085	+53
6335	6285	+ 50	6215	6180	+ 35	6237	6185	+52
6255	6185	+ 70	6037	6000	+ 37	6052	6025	+27
6252	6225	+27	6030	6025	++5	6217	6225	– 8
6290	6275	+15	6090	6110	– 20	6137	6120	+17
6275	6270	+ 5	6155	6130	+ 25	6165	6177	–12
6190	6210	–20	6080	6120	– 40	6095	6142	–47
6295	6342	– 47	6130	6160	– 30	6295	6342	–47
6495	6542	–47	6380	6475	– 95	6420	6480	– 60
6405	6590	–185	6317	6465	– 148	6345	6560	– 215
6545	6760	–215	6305	6495	– 190	6545	6760	– 215
6720	6960	–240	6545	6765	–220	6690	6862	– 172
6735	6980	–245	6610	6830	– 220	6702	6850	–148
6902	7050	–148	6730	6950	– 220	6902	7050	–148
7010	7210	–200	6702	6850	– 148	6702	6360	–158
6740	7000	–260	6540	6760	– 220	6552	6765	–213
6635	6890	–255	6390	6610	– 220	6477	6615	–138
6580	6790	–210	6475	6655	– 180	6482	6657	–175
6682	6857	–175	6460	6640	–180	6537	6670	–133
6510	6720	– 210	6402	6605	– 203	6500	6650	–150
6555	6700	–145	6430	6590	–160	6485	6600	–115
6675	6800	–125	6455	6650	–195	6617	6760	–143
6630	6795	–165	6520	6670	– 250	6527	6677	–150
6500	6650	–150	6327	6550	–223	6390	6570	–180
6430	6630	–200	6300	6510	– 210	6305	6515	–210
6387	6640	– 253	6235	6430	– 195	6377	6542	–165
6430	6650	–220	6275	6520	–245	6345	6540	–195

49

MAR 84 BELLIES VS JULY 84 BELLIES

MAR HIGH	JULY HIGH	DIFF HIGH	MAR LOW	JULY LOW	DIFF LOW	MAR LAST	JULY LAST	DIFF LAST
6375	6560	-185	6165	6445	-280	6187	6460	-273
6305	6575	-270	6110	6410	-300	6297	6555	-258
6372	6640	-268	6260	6535	-275	6275	6557	-282
6342	6610	-268	6265	6550	-285	6317	6562	-245
6515	6762	-247	6320	6590	-270	6507	6740	-233
6525	6780	-255	6440	6700	-260	6477	6727	-250
6460	6750	-110	6277	6590	-313	6315	6600	-285
6360	6640	-280	6220	6530	-310	6235	6530	-295
6295	6600	-305	6170	6485	-315	6240	6485	-245
6270	6540	-270	6210	6465	-255	6217	6467	-250
6200	6465	-265	6050	6350	-300	6055	6357	-302
6150	6450	-300	6025	6340	-315	6092	6415	-323
5990	6335	-345	5900	6255	-355	5940	6272	-332
6010	6330	-320	5910	6240	-330	5992	6320	-328
6000	6350	-350	5880	6217	-337	5937	6257	-320

50

DEC 83 T-BILLS VS DEC 84 T-BILLS

83 HIGH	84 HIGH	DIFF HIGH	83 LOW	84 LOW	DIFF LOW	83 LAST	84 LAST	DIFF LAST
9074	9013	+61	9053	9003	+50	9058	9003	+55
9084	9019	+65	9061	9003	+58	9076	9004	+72
9073	9006	+67	9064	9002	+62	9071	9004	+67
9079	9009	+70	9063	9009	+54	9072	9009	+63
9085	9013	+72	9074	9013	+61	9084	9013	+71
9090	9009	+81	9072	9009	+63	9073	9009	+64
9070	8994	+76	9045	8994	+61	9046	8994	+52
9060	9002	+58	9036	9002	+34	9059	9002	+57
9064	9004	+60	9052	8997	+55	9058	9001	+57
9065	8998	+67	9050	8998	+52	9060	8998	+62
9057	8995	+62	9044	8986	+58	9046	8987	+59
9054	8992	+62	9042	8985	+57	9043	8983	+60
9062	8997	+65	9050	8994	+56	9055	8997	+58
9068	9000	+68	9057	8996	+61	9063	9000	+63
9082	9012	+70	9069	9012	+57	9073	9012	+61
9082	9013	+69	9072	9013	+59	9078	9013	+65
90.48	8983	+65	9038	8992	+56	9039	8984	+55
90.48	8986	+62	9040	8984	+56	9045	8984	+61
9037	8975	+62	9024	8971	+53	9031	8975	+56
9035	8976	+59	9020	8960	+60	9021	8960	+61
9036	8971	+65	9024	8969	+55	9030	8970	+60
9031	8970	+61	9015	8959	+56	9018	8959	+59
9023	8957	+66	9013	8955	+58	9017	8956	+61
9032	8962	+60	9016	8949	+67	9017	8962	+55
9014	8945	+69	9004	8934	+70	9007	8938	+69
9019	8949	+70	9005	8949	+56	9018	8949	+69
9028	8954	+75	9015	8953	+62	9022	8953	+69
9050	8975	+75	9035	8970	+65	9036	8970	+66
9039	8967	+72	9029	8961	+68	9035	8962	+73

51

DEC 83 T-BILLS VS DEC 84 T-BILLS

83 HIGH	84 HIGH	DIFF HIGH	83 LOW	84 LOW	DIFF LOW	83 LAST	84 LAST	DIFF LAST
9032	8959	+73	9020	8950	+70	9023	8950	+73
9035	8958	+77	9013	8946	+67	9034	8958	+76
9035	8957	+78	9028	8953	+75	9029	8953	+76
9035	8956	+79	9028	8951	+77	9029	8951	+78
9030	8951	+79	9013	8936	+77	9014	8938	+76
9017	8937	+80	8997	8921	+76	9004	8926	+78
9004	8926	+78	8990	8916	+74	8995	8916	+79
8995	8914	+81	8982	8910	+72	8990	8913	+77
9005	8932	+73	8988	8921	+67	9002	8932	+70
9007	8928	+79	8982	8916	+66	8983	8916	+67
8985	8915	+70	8977	8914	+63	8980	8915	+65
8977	8910	+67	8967	8902	+65	8976	8903	+73
8985	8908	+77	8975	8908	+67	8982	8908	+74
8981	8902	+79	8973	8900	+73	8980	8901	+79
8988	8912	+76	8980	8908	+72	8986	8912	+74
8996	8922	+74	8989	8917	+72	8992	8920	+72
9016	8941	+75	9006	8935	+71	9013	8939	+74
9029	8958	+71	9010	8945	+65	9025	8957	+68
9038	8964	+74	9028	8959	+69	9036	8963	+73
9041	8968	+73	9028	8963	+65	9029	8964	+65
9031	8965	+66	9020	8949	+71	9021	8949	+72
9050	8973	+77	9038	8966	+72	9046	8967	+79
9047	8969	+78	9036	8958	+78	9039	8960	+79
9054	8970	+84	9043	8963	+80	9045	8964	+81
9057	8973	+84	9032	8954	+78	9033	8954	+79
9035	8954	+81	9024	8944	+80	9032	8954	+78
9018	8939	+79	9007	8926	+81	9008	8927	+81
9020	8934	+86	9005	8927	+78	9010	8927	+83
9017	8930	+87	9001	8920	+81	9008	8924	+84

DEC 83 T-BILLS VS DEC 84 T-BILLS

83 HIGH	84 HIGH	DIFF HIGH	83 LOW	84 LOW	DIFF LOW	83 LAST	84 LAST	DIFF LAST
9022	8934	+88	9012	8924	+88	9016	8924	+92
9015	8925	+90	9012	8921	+91	9013	8922	+91
9040	8943	+97	9029	8939	+90	9031	8939	+92
9050	8961	+89	9026	8943	+83	9049	8961	+88
9055	8964	+91	9043	8958	+85	9044	8958	+86
9050	8962	+88	9045	8961	+84	9046	8962	+84
9078	8990	+88	9064	8977	+87	9067	8977	+90
9072	8985	+87	9062	8976	+86	9066	8976	+90
9064	8973	+91	9054	8960	+94	9055	8962	+93
9058	8964	+94	9047	8957	+90	9057	8957	+94
9069	8971	+98	9053	8965	+88	9066	8969	+97
9088	8989	+99	9068	8975	+93	9075	8976	+99
9089	8989	+100	9079	8987	+92	9083	8987	+96
9089	8994	+95	9079	8985	+94	9082	8987	+95
9088	8992	+96	9073	8979	+94	9087	8991	+96
9100	9000	+100	9093	8991	+102	9097	8992	+105
9114	9007	+107	9104	9001	+103	9112	9003	+109
9110	9001	+109	9103	8993	+110	9108	8993	+115
9114	9000	+114	9098	8990	+108	9100	8991	+109
9105	8996	+109	9093	8985	+108	9104	8996	+108
9114	9002	+112	9105	8999	+106	9112	9002	+110
9113	9003	+110	9104	8999	+105	9107	9000	+107
9118	9009	+109	9103	8999	+104	9111	9003	+108
9128	9014	+114	9116	9007	+109	9126	8954	+172
9130	9017	+113	9123	9013	+110	9126	9013	+113
9126	9014	+112	9116	9010	+106	9121	9014	+107
9113	9009	+104	9105	9002	+103	9106	9009	+97
9107	9005	+102	9088	9001	+87	9090	9001	+89
9096	9008	+88	9084	9000	+84	9092	9004	+88

53

DEC 83 MEAL VS DEC 83 OIL

MEAL HIGH	OIL HIGH	DIFF HIGH	MEAL LOW	OIL LOW	DIFF LOW	MEAL LAST	OIL LAST	DIFF LAST
12140	14928	-2788	12063	14328	-2265	12136	14928	-2792
12190	15504	-3314	12155	15072	-2917	12168	15360	-3192
12255	15870	-3615	12165	15330	-3165	12252	15702	-3450
12270	16140	-3870	12210	15720	-3510	12232	15888	-3656
12310	16488	-4178	12222	15660	-3438	12297	16488	-4191
12340	16800	-4460	12238	16230	-3992	12263	16332	-4069
12285	16488	-4203	12245	16080	-3835	12273	16128	-3855
12373	16728	-4355	12300	16350	-4050	12373	16728	-4355
12440	17148	-4708	12373	16794	-4421	12437	17106	-4669
12520	17706	-5186	12415	17010	-4595	12485	17610	-5125
12585	18210	-5625	12515	18000	-5485	12585	18210	-5625
12685	18810	-6125	12485	18240	-5755	12590	18810	-6220
12600	19230	-6630	12505	18630	-6125	12550	18882	-6332
12505	18750	-6245	12450	18282	-5832	12450	18282	-5832
12425	18120	-5695	12355	17760	-5405	12362	17952	-5590
12462	18552	-6090	12462	18552	-6090	12462	18552	-6090
12562	19152	-6590	12510	19152	-6642	12562	19152	-6590
12590	19752	-7162	12525	19170	-6645	12562	19752	-7190
12662	20652	-7990	12550	19860	-7310	12573	20358	-7785
12565	21258	-8693	12510	19680	-7170	12543	21162	-8619
12535	21270	-8735	12443	20430	-7987	12443	20820	-8377
12400	20580	-8180	12343	20220	-7877	12343	20220	-7877
12430	20700	-8270	12320	19920	-7600	12422	20202	-7780
12455	20490	-8035	12322	19602	-7280	12353	19602	-7249
12453	20010	-7557	12375	19260	-6885	12453	19890	-7437
12540	20250	-7710	12475	19680	-7205	12532	20130	-7598
12550	20520	-7970	12475	20070	-7595	12493	20400	-7907
12490	20640	-8150	12457	20280	-7823	12481	20562	-8081
12559	21162	-8603	12520	20910	-8390	12547	21162	-8615

DEC 83 MEAL VS DEC 83 SOYBEAN OIL

MEAL HIGH	OIL HIGH	DIFF HIGH	MEAL LOW	OIL LOW	DIFF LOW	MEAL LAST	OIL LAST	DIFF LAST	
12540	21540	−9000	12485	21030	−8545	12488	21492	−9004	
12579	22092	−9513	12388	21672	−9284	12388	21738	−9350	
12390	21690	−9300	12300	21138	−8838	12315	21138	−8823	
12353	20958	−8605	12225	20538	−8313	12232	20538	−8306	
12332	20400	−8068	12225	19938	−7713	12332	19962	−7630	
12427	20862	−8435	12345	20340	−7995	12410	20862	−8452	
12435	20910	−8475	12360	20310	−7950	12387	20640	−8253	
12487	21540	−9053	12487	21540	−9053	12487	21540	−9053	

DEC 83 SWISS FRANCS VS DEC 83 D-MARK

SW. FR. HIGH	D.MARK HIGH	DIFF HIGH	SW. FR. LOW	D.MARK LOW	DIFF LOW	SW. FR. LAST	D.MARK LAST	DIFF LAST
4934	4063	871	4910	4045	865	4921	4056	865
4930	4065	865	4869	4022	847	4871	4022	849
4895	4026	869	4845	4006	839	4849	4006	843
4884	4025	859	4859	4010	849	4863	4011	852
4881	4022	859	4855	4010	845	4866	4014	852
4876	4024	852	4860	4016	844	4867	4019	848
4826	3983	843	4804	3969	835	4805	3976	829
4823	3981	842	4813	3974	839	4819	3978	841
4846	3978	868	4784	3955	829	4839	3978	861
4828	3971	857	4810	3961	849	4813	3961	852
4844	3962	882	4804	3947	857	4831	3954	877
4857	3952	905	4822	3940	882	4842	3947	895
4860	3957	903	4830	3941	889	4841	3955	886
4854	3967	887	4826	3949	877	4827	3949	878
4823	3931	892	4804	3921	883	4809	3922	887
4835	3942	893	4824	3930	894	4832	3935	897
4835	3943	892	4821	3931	890	4823	3936	888
4904	3974	930	4867	3958	909	4895	3971	924
4903	3972	931	4867	3945	922	4872	3945	927
4876	3949	927	4848	3930	918	4862	3941	921
4842	3921	921	4822	3905	917	4836	3916	920
4859	3922	937	4835	3905	930	4839	3913	926
4841	3896	945	4825	3887	938	4825	3890	935
4821	3888	933	4804	3871	933	4806	3872	934
4802	3861	941	4740	3834	906	4746	3839	908
4757	3828	929	4729	3798	931	4749	3814	935
4780	3837	943	4760	3825	935	4772	3829	943
4764	3832	932	4737	3825	912	4749	3829	920
4758	3840	918	4720	3807	913	4722	3809	913

56

DEC 83 SWISS FRANCS VS DEC 83 D-MARK

SW. FR. HIGH	D.MARK HIGH	DIFF HIGH	SW.FR. LOW	D.MARK LOW	DIFF LOW	SW.FR. LAST	D.MARK LAST	DIFF LAST
4715	3803	912	4693	3778	915	4704	3794	910
4698	3789	909	4674	3768	906	4697	3787	910
4704	3791	913	4674	3774	900	4678	3775	903
4663	3750	913	4646	3725	921	4651	3729	922
4669	3727	942	4648	3710	938	4657	3712	945
4693	3740	953	4659	3724	935	4685	3738	947
4764	3792	972	4695	3742	953	4755	3784	971
4779	3822	957	4729	3791	938	4739	3804	935

DEC 83 T-BONDS VS DEC 83 GNMA

BONDS HIGH	GNMA HIGH	DIFF HIGH	BONDS LOW	GNMA LOW	DIFF LOW	BONDS LAST	GNMA LAST	DIFF LAST
7407	6717	+6.20	7315	6700	6.15	7400	6715	6.17
7422	6803	6.19	7331	6718	613	7402	6723	6.11
7408	6723	617	7328	6715	613	7401	6720	613
7417	6730	619	7323	6713	610	7415	6729	607
7424	6809	6.15	7329	6711	618	7400	6715	617
7403	6717	6.18	7315	6631	616	7320	6702	618
7408	6718	622	7325	6703	622	7402	6707	627
7412	6713	631	7328	6703	625	7400	6705	627
7502	6800	702	7409	6713	628	7500	6800	700
7431	6802	629	7418	6722	628	7423	6731	623
7508	6816	624	7414	6728	618	7504	6813	623
7524	6830	626	7503	6813	622	7521	6828	625
7525	6830	627	7507	6813	626	7511	6817	626
7514	6816	630	7422	6729	625	7424	6730	626
7426	6730	628	7409	6715	626	7426	6730	628
7428	6809	619	7413	6726	619	7417	6731	618
7420	6801	619	7330	6718	612	7414	6729	617
7411	6724	619	7312	6703	609	7315	6705	610
7324	6709	615	7221	6601	610	7226	6608	618
7318	6628	622	7302	6612	622	7306	6623	615
7324	6706	618	7309	6620	621	7320	6705	615
7405	6717	620	7324	6703	621	7329	6707	622
7401	6709	624	7327	6704	623	7331	6706	625
7229	6607	622	7203	6519	616	7210	6527	615
7223	6608	615	7210	6529	613	7219	6604	615
7208	6530	610	7123	6511	612	7200	6526	606
7205	6600	605	7113	6511	602	7115	6512	603
7209	6603	606	7126	6520	606	7130	6527	603
7131	6528	603	7102	6515	520	7105	6521	515

DEC 83 T-BONDS VS DEC 83 GNMA

6/1/83

BONDS	GNMA	DIFF	BONDS	GNMA	DIFF	BONDS	GNMA	DIFF
HIGH	HIGH	HIGH	LOW	LOW	LOW	LAST	LAST	LAST
7119	6706	4.13	7031	6519	5.12	7109	6616	4.25
7205	6727	4.10	7112	6626	4.18	7117	6718	3.31
7114	6728	3.18	7024	6707	3.17	7107	6714	325
7131	6800	3.31	7109	6719	3.22	7131	6800	3.31
7212	6809	4.03	7127	6727	4.00	7203	6905	330
7311	6907	4.04	7212	6806	4.06	7203	6811	324
7215	6815	4.00	7130	6728	4.02	7131	6731	4.00
7130	6727	4.03	7030	6709	3.21	7105	6711	+3.26

59

FEB 84 CATTLE VS JUNE 84 LIVE CATTLE

FEB HIGH	JUNE HIGH	DIFF HIGH	FEB LOW	JUNE LOW	DIFF LOW	FEB LAST	JUNE LAST	DIFF LAST
5945	6177	-232	5895	6155	-260	5930	6075	-145
5955	6190	-235	5855	6110	-255	5855	6130	-275
5950	6185	-235	5915	6185	-210	5937	6185	-248
5935	6187	-252	5912	6165	-253	5912	6187	-275
5955	6212	-257	5900	6185	-285	5910	6212	-302
5955	6225	-270	5880	6180	-300	5895	6195	-300
6045	6345	-300	5900	6212	-312	6045	6345	-300
6100	6395	-295	6030	6340	-310	6047	6385	-338
6097	6377	-280	6005	6350	-345	6075	6377	-302
6210	6420	-210	6045	6347	-302	6205	6410	-205
6200	6420	-220	6175	6360	-185	6190	6420	-230
6180	6410	-230	6115	6370	-255	6152	6387	-235
6240	6465	-225	6187	6400	-213	6202	6450	-248
6225	6450	-225	6160	6400	-240	6185	6415	-230
6210	6450	-240	6170	6397	-227	6197	6442	-245
6200	6445	-245	6152	6425	-273	6157	6430	-273
6232	6510	-278	6195	6440	-255	6195	6450	-255
6200	6470	-270	6155	6445	-290	6190	6465	-275
6272	6550	-278	6190	6450	-260	6267	6550	-283
6320	6580	-260	6245	6507	-262	6257	6535	-278
6287	6535	-248	6250	6500	-250	6262	6535	-273
6345	6585	-240	6250	6535	-285	6292	6575	-283
6310	6585	-275	6240	6530	-290	6277	6552	-275
6297	6540	-243	6235	6507	-272	6285	6527	-242
6350	6595	-245	6305	6570	-265	6317	6590	-273
6355	6655	-300	6205	6510	-305	6207	6520	-313
6207	6507	-300	6105	6410	-305	6110	6437	-327
6122	6442	-320	6075	6390	-315	6082	6422	-340
6120	6445	-325	6087	6400	-313	6092	6420	-328

60

FEB 84 LIVE CATTLE VS JUNE 84 LIVE CATTLE

FEB HIGH	JUNE HIGH	DIFF HIGH	FEB LOW	JUNE LOW	DIFF LOW	FEB LAST	JUNE LAST	DIFF LAST
6165	6520	-355	6050	6410	-360	6070	6450	-380
6100	6485	-385	6055	6435	-380	6085	6480	-395
6100	6477	-377	6012	6420	-408	6020	6430	-410
6075	6497	-422	5995	6427	-432	6065	6470	-405
6085	6485	-400	6040	6440	-400	6052	6462	-410
6035	6460	-425	5925	6360	-435	5930	6362	-432
5975	6375	-400	5910	6325	-415	5965	6355	-390
5965	6355	-390	5880	6295	-415	5890	6325	-435
5942	6370	-428	5892	6330	-438	5932	6342	-410
5925	6350	-425	5830	6300	-470	5840	6305	-465
5990	6455	-465	5850	6325	-475	5987	6452	-465
6050	6490	-440	5985	6430	-445	5990	6460	-470
6040	6470	-430	5990	6435	-445	5997	6452	-455
6075	6520	-445	6017	6465	-448	6070	6505	-435
6140	6540	-400	6065	6495	-430	6137	6532	-395
6115	6530	-415	6025	6455	-430	6062	6490	-428
6087	6500	-413	6027	6442	-415	6055	6475	-420
6120	6525	-405	6050	6470	-420	6090	6480	-390
6140	6515	-375	6095	6470	-375	6132	6507	-375
6115	6505	-390	6057	6452	-395	6085	6487	-402
6085	6475	-390	6035	6430	-435	6055	6450	-395
6105	6545	-440	6005	6425	-395	6100	6515	-415
6195	6570	-375	6120	6505	-385	6185	6565	-380
6200	6562	-362	6160	6515	-385	6187	6547	-360
6215	6570	-355	6155	6525	-370	6187	6557	-370
6197	6550	-353	6140	6512	-372	6185	6542	-357

61

Chapter 7

How To Scale
The Twin-Line Graph

I use two types of chart paper for graphing twin-line spreads. They are manufactured by Keuffel & Esser Corp. The chart intended for grain spreads is coded #1650. Spreads other than the grains are graphed on type 1320 paper. Either sheet can be purchased at most any stationery, art supply or engineering supply house. Due to publishing considerations the graph paper used in the examples in this book is neither of those two types.

A few spreads can be graphed with equal ease on either sheet, in particular those spreads having a point value computed in 32nds. (i.e.—T-Bonds and/or GNMA spreads).

Semi-log or logorithmic chart paper cannot be used at all because the horizontal lines are not equidistant from one another.

When you scale a spread graph, which includes a zero line to split plus and minus differentials, remember that each horizontal line must have the same value increment above and below the zero line.

Suppose you are doing a bond spread and you assign a value to each line of two points and then calculate a spread difference of one (falling between the two lines). Where should it be placed? Quite simply it should be placed an equidistance between the value of line 1 and line 2. As a matter of fact, you will have to gauge where to place the spread difference. This, however, should present no problem.

Vertical lines denote time. Each vertical line contains one day's data. Do not skip a line because of weekends, holidays, etc. All lines are used, there should be no breaks in the graph.

As you gain experience, you will assign your own values to the horizontal lines. For now you can use these values:

All grain spreads (except soybeans): ¼ cent per line.
Bean spreads (intra): ¼ cent. Bean Spreads (Inter): ½ cent.
Meat spreads (cattle, hogs): 5 to 10 points per line.
Sugar: 2 pts. Coffee: 10 pts. Cocoa: 5 to 10 pts.
Orange Juice: 10 pts. Lumber or Plywood: 20 pts.
Cotton: 10 pts. per line.
International currencies: 5 pts.
Stock indexes: 5 pts.
Financial instruments: 2 pts.
Spreads requiring money values be used: $10.00/$20.00 per line.

At the top of the graph you'll find the month and year of each contract, as well as the date you started to plot the spread. To the left, just above the top line to be scaled, you insert (in caps) the value assigned to each line. It should stand out in bold relief.

Do not place a value next to each horizontal line. The numbers will be too close together. Incorrect posting is often the result of glutting up the scale with too many numbers. Place a value next to each fourth or fifth line.

You will need at least two, preferably three, lead pencils using a size .05mm lead. After much trial and error I found this size lead best for my work.

At this point I must make mention of an important fact. I am about to describe exactly how to plot the twin-line graph. Then, in a few lines, I will present an alternate procedure for deriving these graphs. Due to publishing considerations, the graphs reproduced in this book have been done using the alternate procedure. Just be aware of the fact that ''the blue line'' and ''the solid line'' refer to the same line; one of the two lines on the chart. ''The red line'' and the dotted line also refer to the same line; the second of two lines on the chart (distinctly different from the blue/solid line from the previous sentence). In keeping with the way the charts are presented, I will be referring to solid and dotted lines (not blue and red lines) throughout this text. This is merely for easy reference and simpler reading and should not influence the way you maintain your charts. In fact I often use the "colored pencil" method rather than the alternate procedure used here in the book. This may be a little confusing now but in a few paragraphs you will completely understand what I've just described.

The highest spread differential is plotted using a red pencil. The low spread difference is plotted with a blue pencil. A black pencil is used for drawing trend lines.

Each day the red dot is connected to the previous day's difference, resulting in a red line. You do the same thing for the low using blue. The result is that you have two lines; red for the high and blue for the low.

Always use one color for the high line and the second color for the low line. This is important because they, more than anything else, highlight bull and bear spread signals.

ALTERNATE PROCEDURE

There are two ways to graph spreads based on the methodology espoused in this work. The first is to use two lines, each one a different color. I have chosen to use red for the highest spread difference and blue for the second line, the low spread difference. Since I have always graphed using two colors, it never occurred to me that an alternate method could be employed. Yet this second technique is, as a matter of fact, simpler and easier to use:

1. Each day, as you place a dot denoting the highest spread difference, you do not connect the dots, they stand alone.

2. The lowest spread difference is graphed as a solid line, that is, after you place a dot denoting the lowest difference, you simply connect each day's dot to form a solid line.

Since you do not use two colors to designate the high and low range, you will not make errors by inadvertently picking up the wrong color pencil. The signals are the same. (The signals are detailed in the next chapter but are just mentioned here to give you an idea how the li:es you are constructing are used). When the dotted line (high spread difference) goes below a previous low, you put on a bear spread (short the first contract, long the second contract). When the solid line (low spread difference) goes above a previous high (dotted line), you go long the first contract and short the second contract.

Spread trendline penetrations are traded the same as if you had two solid lines. A move above a downsloping trendline indicates a bull spread (long the first contract, short the second contract). A penetration below an up sloping trend line is a signal to put on a bear spread (short the first contract, long the second contract). Trendlines on the graphs are drawn on as solid lines running crosswise across the charts.

Now that you know the how of preparing a graph for posting, it remains for you to develop spread parameters.

OBTAINING SPREAD GRAPH PARAMETERS

Parameters are two spread differentials which will usually encompass future spread values.

1. Find the highest price of each of the contracts to this point in time. Then obtain the spread difference.

2. Find the lowest price of each contract to this point in time. Then obtain the spread difference.

(Note: The highest and lowest contract's price can be obtained through the Wall St. Journal under the columns marked *"Lifetime High Low"* on the commodity page).

You now have the spread differences for each of the contracts. The next step is to check the high/low spread difference for the contracts you intend to graph. If today's spread range is relatively centered between the lifetime high/low spread difference, then simply scale the graph using the lifetime spread differences as the high and low parameters. You will then know that your entry for today will be close to the middle of the graph paper with plenty of room for the spread to move higher and lower.

Suppose today's spread difference is close to its lifetime high or low. How do you proceed to scale the graph so that you have room for higher or lower spread differences? Let's begin by assuming that today's high is close to the contract high.

In this situation you place today's high difference next to the center line on the graph. Then in equal increments above and below the difference, you scale the graph.

Should the low price of today be close to the lifetime spread low, you find the center line and next to it place today's low price. Then, in equal increments scale the graph above and below the price on the center line.

The value you assign to each line on the graph can really be anything you want it to be; as long as each line has an equal increment (value). Earlier I listed values which cover virtually every spread. At this time, you might want to review the assigned values I use.

When you do a spread and notice that the differences are so close together that you cannot see the twin-line signals, simply redo the scale by decreasing the value per line.

Should the graph be too wide, increase the value per line. This will have the effect of tightening your work.

Also please be aware that many graphs will go below a zero line and negative spread differences come into play. Simply incorporate a negative region of values on your scale.

HOW MANY SPREADS TO GRAPH

The number of twin-line spreads you should be graphing depends on three factors: (1) the time available you can devote, (2) the number of spreads expected to crest or make a low within the next couple of months and, (3) your spread trading capital.

It takes a minute or so to obtain the high low spread difference and another 30 seconds to graph the results and graph them onto the twin-line graph.

Once your graphing chores are done, it remains for you to study each graph for possible trading signals. This should take you no more than a half hour or so. As you gain experience, your charting time is reduced.

Chapter 8

Understanding The
Twin-Line Spread Graph

TWIN-LINE SPREAD GRAPH SIGNALS

Following is an outline of the twin-line spread graph signals. There are eight possible courses of action with the twin-line method:

Long (Bull) Spreads

1) When the solid line (denoting the spread's daily low differential) goes above a previous recent high (a high that has occurred within the past 7 charted days) which is denoted by the dotted line, two courses of action are suggested:

    (a) Put on a bull spread the next day, or

    (b) If you are in a bear spread, offset and reverse the position.

2. Upon a penetration of a spread above a down sloping trendline (a down sloping trendline is one moving from upper left to lower right; a thorough description of trendlines and their construction is presented later in this book) two courses of action are suggested:

    (a) Put on a bull spread the next day, or

    (b) If you are in a bear spread, offset and reverse the position.

Short (Bear) Spreads

1. When the dotted line (denoting the spread's daily high differential) goes below a previous recent low (a low that has occurred within the previous 7 days) denoted by the solid line, two courses of action are suggested:

    (a) Put on a bear spread the next day, or

    (b) If you are in a bull spread, offset and reverse the position.

2. Upon a penetration of a spread below an upsloping trendline (an upsloping trendline is one moving from lower left to upper right), two courses of action are suggested:

    (a) Put on a bear spread the next day, or

    (b) If you are in a bull spread, offset and reverse.

Each of the eight possibilities just mentioned will be explained in depth as we work through this chapter.

You'll notice quite often that when a trendline break occurs, a simultaneous twin-line signal will develop. If not at the same time, then within a period of 3 to 5 days. You must, in a sense, "program" yourself to act on all signals—whether it's a trendline break or twin-line signal. They both are legitimate signals requiring an action to be taken on your part.

Shortly we are going to graph a few twin-line examples. Each day, as I post the high and low spread difference, I will spell out the steps I am taking. However, before I go into the examples, there are a few other topics that must first be examined. First, we'll look at stops and I will show you my unconventional but effective stop procedure which involves the use of twin-line signals and trendlines. Then, in a section on trendline construction, I will show you how to go about placing trendlines on your twin-line charts.

STOPS

The stops I use are not the traditional price stops you are accustomed to seeing. Traditional stop placement involves the selection of a specific price by a trader (or is dictated to the trader by a trading system). If the price movement of a commodity touches the trader's stop price level, the trader usually closes out his position and absorbs a loss, or gets out of his position and takes a position in the opposite direction (a stop and reverse).

Traditional stop placement is much more prevalent when the trader is holding on outright open position rather than when in a spread. The protection and safety afforded the trader by a spread position makes the use of stops less essential although they are often applied to prevent a spread from moving against you.

There are a number of problems I find with traditional price stop placement. I will mention a few of these here and then present "stops" as they are used with my method.

In placing traditional stops, it is very difficult to select the optimal price to locate the stop. While there is no magic formula that can tell you the perfect location, commodity traders as a whole tend to place their stops too close to the present price action resulting in premature offsetting. Having stops too close to the price action is usually due to fear of losing money and a lack of confidence in the procedures used to determine the original position taken.

A second problem with traditional stop placement is the "bunching" of stops at a particular price level. Certain popular trading techniques spell out the same stop for all traders applying the technique. This bunching waves a flag to the floor trader who very often can influence price sufficiently to take out all the traders with those particular stops in place, before having price resume its natural course. Very often price will head in the direction you had originally speculated it would, but now, instead of profiting from it, you are on the sidelines wishing you had placed your stop just one tick further away. To some this may sound like a paranoid scenario of some frustrated trader, but it simply is not. It is an example of how the human element comes into play in commodity trading rendering traditional stop placement useless in many instances.

The twin-line method, rather than using traditional price stops, relies on two indices to put on and offset positions. Most methods you've probably come across involve one index which recommend a position be taken, with a stop placed close to the current price level. Twin-line, instead, uses two indices (the twin-line signals and the trendline penetrations) which more efficiently call the direction the spread will be taking and spell out if and when the time has come to reverse your spread position. By using two indices to stay on the winning side of the spread, and by not having to rely on nervously placed "too close" price stops, the trader is kept in the market when he should be in the market and is correct in his trading more often.

71

The two indices, twin-line signals and trendline penetrations, were discussed earlier in this chapter and won't be repeated here. Suffice it to say that on a daily basis you must check your charts to see if a new twin-line signal has been given or if a trendline has been penetrated (trendline construction will be discussed momentarily). Checking daily if either or both of these indices has signaled a change in your spread position will be superior to the use of specific price stop placement for our purposes.

Before going on to a discussion of trendline construction I would just like to present two items which are essential for you to understand in order to have a complete working knowledge of the twin-line method. The items involve trendline penetrations and are included in this section because, as I mentioned above, a trendline penetration is one of the two indices you must be checking for, and can be considered a "stop" of sorts as I use them.

Item 1: When *either* the high or low price line on a twin-line graph penetrates the trendline, the offset and reverse signal is activated.

Item 2: If a trendline penetration occurs one day and then breaks the trendline in the opposite direction the next day you should do as the rules tell you and offset and reverse the original position on the first day and then offset and reverse that subsequent position the next day. Overnight news or some other effect may cause a penetration which doesn't carry very far, before reversing its direction in line with its movement prior to the penetration. You must just live with this small disturbance and offset and reverse twice.

If these two items are not completely clear right now, remember to refer back to them later once you've had a chance to complete this chapter and work through the examples in the next chapter.

CONSTRUCTING A TRENDLINE

A downsloping trendline cannot be drawn in unless and until two highs (the second below the first) are in place. An upsloping trendline cannot be drawn in unless and until two lows are in place (the second being higher than the first). Now you may wonder, how does a spreader know when a high or low is in place? The answer is simple, you don't know until they are in place. For example, say a spread moves from 60 to 90. When it hits 90, it it may remain at that level for a day, a week or longer before a reaction sets in. The spread may then drop to 60 and the first high is in place. Then it reverses, moving to 80, 85 or higher and stopping below its previous high of 90. From its second high, using 80 as the top, the spread reacts again, trading below 80. Now the second high is in place. You can start your downsloping trendline beginning at the first high of 90 and drawing the line down to the 80 level, continuing as subsequent highs are made which fail to break the earlier two highs.

Following through on this example of confirming when highs are in place, we turn our attention to how to find price lows and connecting these lows to form an upsloping trendline.

The reaction from the high of 90 which was arrested at 60 put our first low in place. In place because at that level the spread reversed direction. When the spread reached 80, another reaction took place. It fell to 70, then rallied back to between 75 and 80. At this point, the second low is in place. Admittedly this example is conveniently constructed to give us both an upsloping and downsloping trendline. That, quite obviously, is not always the case but is presented for instructional purposes.

For the next few pages I will present some of the more common questions about trendline construction which I have encountered and give you my answers within the context of the twin-line method.

Question: Is it possible to actually have two trendlines?

Answer: Yes, but not for very long. What is going to happen is that the downsloping trendline, moving from upper left to lower right is going to converge with the upsloping trendline moving from lower left to upper right. The convergence will form sort of a triangle, from which the price will break out above or below the formation. The direction in which the break-out takes place will determine, not only the position you will be in, but also which trendline is now in effect and which trendline is now obsolete.

Question: How soon after starting a graph should I wait until a trendline should be drawn in?

Answer: There is no specified time factor. Wait until you have two highs and/or lows in place. That can take anywhere from a few days to a couple of weeks.

Question: Do you always use 2 points to start a trendline?

Answer: That is how I've presented the method in this text, however, out of personal preference I sometimes draw my trendlines across three points. For now though, I recommend you use 2 points. Once adept at the twin-line method you may want to test if using three points may improve your trading.

Question: Is it advisable to put on a spread as the price approaches the trendline in anticipation of a trendline penetration?

Answer: Absolutely not. Stick to the rules and wait for a penetration. If you start making exceptions to the rules you will gradually deviate more and more from the original twin-line method and you will eventually find yourself on your own again in an industry which has a very low survival rate. Stick to the rules!

HOW HIGH IS HIGH? HOW LOW IS LOW?

No one knows with certainty. When you get a signal, it is in your best interest to act on it. And stay with the position until such time as an offsetting signal develops. Yes, there will be infrequent times when you'll have to offset a new position resulting in a small loss or breakeven situation. At times, within a few days, a new signal may even put you right back into the original position. The consolation to you is that by following this procedure, when the big move starts, you'll be in on it from the start. Catching the big moves in spread trading is what twin-line does best. This point will be evidenced quite clearly in the next chapter as we look at some examples of twin-line in action.

Chapter 9

Twin-Line Spreading Examples

THE JULY 1984 CORN VS. JULY 1984 OATS SPREAD

I have included the dates on the work form for this spread so as to make it easier for you to follow along. With respect to the graph on this spread, I will refer to certain days in number form (i.e.—Day 16, Day 41, etc.). Each vertical line constitutes one day's trading.

This spread is presented on a day-by-day trading basis. Other spread examples throughout the book will not be quite as specific as to what happened each day. Please go through this example slowly so that you can see exactly how twin-line works since after this point I will assume you will have absorbed the mechanics of my methodology.

Day 1: Today is June 1, 1984. First I must figure out the scale for the graph. Given the space restrictions of my graph paper and knowing the lifetime high and low of the spread, I settle on using a scale of one dollar on the low side and two dollars on the high side. This leaves plenty of room for the spread to move in either direction. I post the high and low spread differential and, understandably, because of the early stages of the spread, there is no action on this date.

Day 2: No action

Day 3: No action

Day 4: A bull signal is nearly given but isn't given. There is still ''no action'' on this date. Even though it is tempting to anticipate a bull signal since the spread's low has equalled the high of two of the past four days, don't do it. Stick to the rules!

Day 5: A bull signal is given to go long the corn and short the oats. The spread should be initiated at tomorrow's open.

Day 6: In at the open receiving a fill at $159.00. Now begin keeping an eye out for a reversal signal. In addition there still isn't enough data to draw in a trendline. Watch and wait.

Day 7: The spread looks good so far. Today's high was at $160.25 and the low was at $160.00. Keep checking for a reversal.

Day 8: No action.

Day 9: Today I drew in my bullish upsloping trendline. I used day one since it is the lowest low and connect it to the low on day 4. That means it will intersect day's 1, 3, and 4. I can't extend the line until a little more data is graphed.

Day 10: No action.

Day 11: No action.

Day 12: I entered the trendline beyond day 10. Today's low difference has taken out the week's lows by moving above them and in so doing has confirmed the validity of the trendline.

Day 13: Today I have a twin-line reversal and a confirming trendline reversal. Tomorrow, I'm going out on the opening and I'll reverse the spread.

Day 14: The opening difference was $158.25. I lost ¾ of a cent from my entry price plus $110.00 commission, for a total of $147.50. Now, I'd better get my trendline up to today's low.

Day 15: No action. Watch and wait.

Day 16: No action. No reversal signal.

Day 17: No action. No reversal signal.

Day 18: The low price today of $152.00 made an upside penetration of the trendline. Tomorrow morning I'm offsetting and reversing the spread.

Day 19: Well, today turned out pretty good. The opening spread difference was $153.25, the exact low for the day. Now I'm long corn/short oats and the closing difference is $156.25, which gives me an accrued profit of $150.00. Let's see what I did on the spread I offset. I went into the short corn/long oats on day 14 at $158.25, out today at $153.25. My profit is $250.00, less $110.00, or $140.00. I'm still out $7.50. At any rate, I received a confirming twin-line signal. Interesting how both signals tend to come at the same time, or close to one another.

Day 20: No action.

Day 21: No action.

Day 22: No action.

Day 23: No action.

Day 24: Since the low went above the previous four day lows which hardly moved, I can extend my trendline.

Day 25: No action.

Day 26: No action.

Day 27: No action.

Day 28: No action.

Day 29: No action.

Day 30: A penetration of today's low is a twin-line signal to offset and reverse. Tommorow that's what I will do at the opening.

Day 31: The opening spread difference is $161.50. I put on the spread at $153.25 on day 19. So in 12 days I made 8¼ cents. Gross Profit $412.50, less $110.00 commission leaves $302.50. Subtract $7.50 from that amount and the net profit is $295.00. Now I'm short the corn/long the oats at $161.50.

Day 32: No action.

Day 33: Tomorrow I'm out and will reverse going out of my long oats/short corn and going long corn/short oats. The twin-line has not reversed, only a one day penetration of the trendline which reversed itself today. Can't fight the tape.

Day 34: Went out at the opening and reversed at a flat $165.00. My loss is 3½ cents or $175.00, plus $110.00 commission equals $285.00.

Day 35: No action. Close was up 2½ cents or $125.00.

Day 36: No action, up another $50.00.

Day 37: No action, up another cent on the close to $169.50.

Day 38: Today the spread closed at $171.50; 2 cents above yesterday. At least now I've got an accrued profit of 6½ cents. A $325.00 profit in 4 days isn't bad.

Day 39: No action.

Day 40: No action.

On March 22, 1984 the close was $171.75. An accrued profit of 6¾ cents or $337.50. There is also a net profit of $10.00. Assume for the moment that the spread was offset. The commission of $110.00 deducted from the gross profit of $337.50, leaves a net of $227.50, plus $10.00 for a total of $237.50.

It is not my intention to try and impress you by playing with numbers. Nevertheless, you should know that the margin required to put on one corn/oats spread is $800.00. If we look at our return of $237.50 as a percent rate of return on the margin, it comes to 29.69% for the 40 days.

Twin-line will keep you in a position until one of two types of reversal signals occur: an actual twin-line signal or a trendline signal telling you to get out. Once in awhile a false signal will develop as happened on day 33 when the spread's low violated the trendline for one day. Take solace in the fact that the loss was small. It could have been worse, much worse. In the final analysis, a methodology to be effective, must first protect your capital and second, give you the signals to take a position. I believe that twin-line fulfills both responsibilities.

JULY 84 COTTON VS. DEC. 84 COTTON

The spread which we will study is the July 1984 vs. Dec. 1984 cotton spread.

Rather than clutter up the graph with dates, I am going to refer to each day's action numerically (i.e.—day 4, 7, 10, 16, etc.). By counting each vertical line as one day (which they are), you'll know exactly the particular point I am discussing.

In my work I assign 5 points per line for cotton. However, in order to highlight the salient points, I shall increase the size of the graph by 2½ times by using 2 points per line. When and if you work with cotton, employ a value of 5 points per line.

We are going to put this spread under a microscope. From day one (and each day thereafter, when appropriate) I shall comment on the unfolding situation.

Day 1: Started spread. High/low range, 10 pts.
Day 2: No action.
Day 3: No action.
Day 4: No action.
Day 5: Bullish signal in effect. Low has gone above high of day 3.

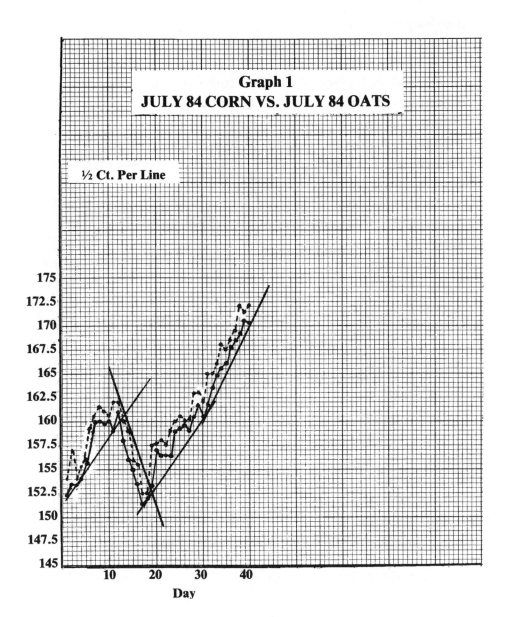

Graph 1
JULY 84 CORN VS. JULY 84 OATS

½ Ct. Per Line

Day

79

Prepare to go long next day.

Day 6: In at 495. Long the July, short the Dec.

Day 7: No action.

Day 8: A reversal took place. Will offset tomorrow and also reverse the position. Since I have a top on day 2 and a top on day 5, I'm going to draw in a downsloping trendline connecting these two tops.

Because the angle was so acute, I am off by about 1/16 of an inch in my effort to connect day 5. The error, being so small, will have no effect on the validity of the line.

Day 9: Offset and reversed on a differential of 448. My loss is 47 points or $235.00 plus a $100.00 commission for a net loss of $335.00. However, I'm now in at 448.

Day 10: I have a top on day 9. Will draw in continuing trendline. Again I'm a little off. However, since the line is between day's 9 and 10, I'll leave it alone.

Note: Keep in mind that when you draw in a trendline slightly off the mark, it will not affect your work. Of course try to draw it as close to the connecting tops (or bottoms) as you can.

Day 11: Spread is in a free fall, so I'll sit back and enjoy it.

Day 12: No action.

Day 13: Spread made a low of 262. Since the action is almost straight down, I'm unable to continue the trendline. Will just have to wait and see what hapens.

Day 14: No action.

Day 15: Very interesting. The low was 305, a scant 4 points away from going one point above the high of 308 recorded on day 13.

Day 16: I have my reversal signal. Tomorrow I'll close the spread and reverse.

Day 17: Out at 343. Am now in a bull spread at the same time. On day 9, I was in a bear spread at 448, so my profit is 105 points or $525.00. Subtracting the commission of $100.00 plus a realized loss of $335.00 for a total of $435.00, leaves me with a profit of $90.00.

Day 18: Now I can draw in the trendline to the top of day 17.

Day 19: Today I have a double long signal. The high of 385 penetrated the trendline, and the low of 335 reconfirmed the bull twin-line signal on day 15 which caused me to put on a bull spread on day 16.

Day 20: This spread is moving up as fast as it fell! Nothing to do now except to draw in an upsloping trendline connecting the bottom of day 13 to the low made on day 18.

Day 21: I see I have the same problem with the upsloping trendline as I had with the downsloping one. The spread is moving so far and so fast that I'm unable to continue the new trendline. The only thing to do is wait.

Day 22: Still moving up.

Day 23: No action.

Day 24: No action.

Day 25: No action.

Day 26: No action other than now I can connect the low made on day 25.

Day 27: No action.

Day 28: A trendline downside break occurred today. I will offset and reverse the spread. In addition, I can now draw in a downsloping trendline connecting the top on day 22 with the double top made on day's 26 and 27.

Day 29: Out at 480 on the bull spread and in on a bear spread at the same price. Let's see, I put on the bull trade at 343 on day 17 after a reversal the day before. My profit is 137 points or $685.00. With my previous profit of $90.00, my gross is $775.00. Subtracting the $100.00 commission, my net profit is $665.00.

Day 30: A reversal occurred today when the high price slammed through my declining tops trendline. Tomorrow I close and put on a bull spread.

Day 31: Out and in at 550. Loss is 70 points or $350.00 plus $100.00 commission for a total of $450.00. New profit is now $215.00. I'm now in a bull spread at 550.

Day 32: No action.

Day 33: No action.

Day 34: No action.

Day 35: Just two points separating the high and low, 619 versus 617.

Day 36: Signal to offset and reverse from a bull spread to a bear spread tomorrow.

Day 37: Offset at 579 and put on a bear spread at the same difference. Since I went in at 550 on day 31, my profit of 29 points or $145.00 is what I made less $100.00 commission for a profit of $45.00. This added to my profit of $215.00 equals $260.00.

Day 38: No action.

Day 39: A trendline was drawn in from the low of day 29 connecting the low of day 39.

Day 40: Offset and reverse position.

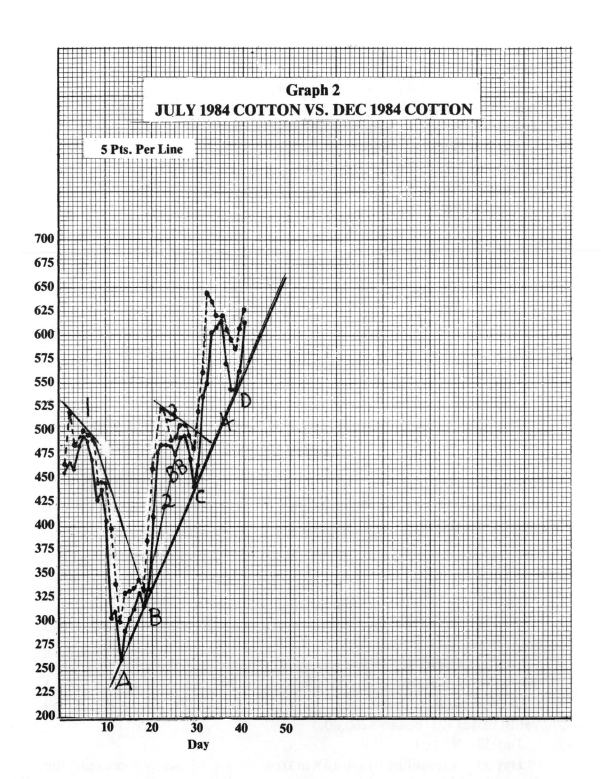

Graph 2
JULY 1984 COTTON VS. DEC 1984 COTTON

5 Pts. Per Line

Day

THE NOVEMBER 1984 VS. MARCH 1985 ORANGE JUICE SPREAD

Overview

During a recent 24 day period, commencing May 1, 1984, three orange juice spread positions were put on and offset. A net return on equity (margin) amounted to 32%.

While I could have continued trading orange juice, until close to the "spot" month, it would have served no purpose as far as your training is concerned. The central point to keep in mind is to always wait for a signal, whether it is a twin-line signal or a trendline penetration.

When trading spreads through a discount firm, your commissions are 50% less. Thus, profits will be larger and losses smaller.

Day 1: Started spread.

Day 2: No action.

Day 3: No action.

Day 4: Bear signal. Will take a position on day 5.

Day 5: Went in at a plus 270 points.

Day 6: No action.

Day 7: No action.

Day 8: No action.

Day 9: Reversal signal. Will offset and reverse on day 10.

*Day 10: Offset bear spread, then went the other way by going long Nov./short March at a plus 185 points.

*Profit 85 points or $127.50 (point value $1.50). Commission of $100.00 resulted in a net profit of $27.50.

Day 11: A one day reversal occurred today. Will offset long spread tomorrow.

*Day 12: Reversed at a plus 245 points, expecting the spread to move lower.

*Profit 60 points (or $90.00). Commission $100.00. Net loss $10.00.

Day 13: No action.

Day 14: No action.

Day 15: No action.

Day 16: No action.

Day 17: No action.

Day 18: No action.

Twin-Line Spreading Examples

Day 19: No action.
Day 20: No action.
Day 21: No action.
Day 22: No action.
Day 23: Reversal signal. Will close out the position tomorrow.
Day 24: Offset but did not reverse at a plus 30 points. Profit 215 points ($322.50). Commission $100.00. Net Profit $222.50.

Recap:

Trade 1-	Profit	$ 27.50
Trade 2-	Loss	$ 10.00
Trade 3-	Profit	$222.50
Net profit-		$240.00
Margin-		$750.00
% Return-		32%
Time-		24 days

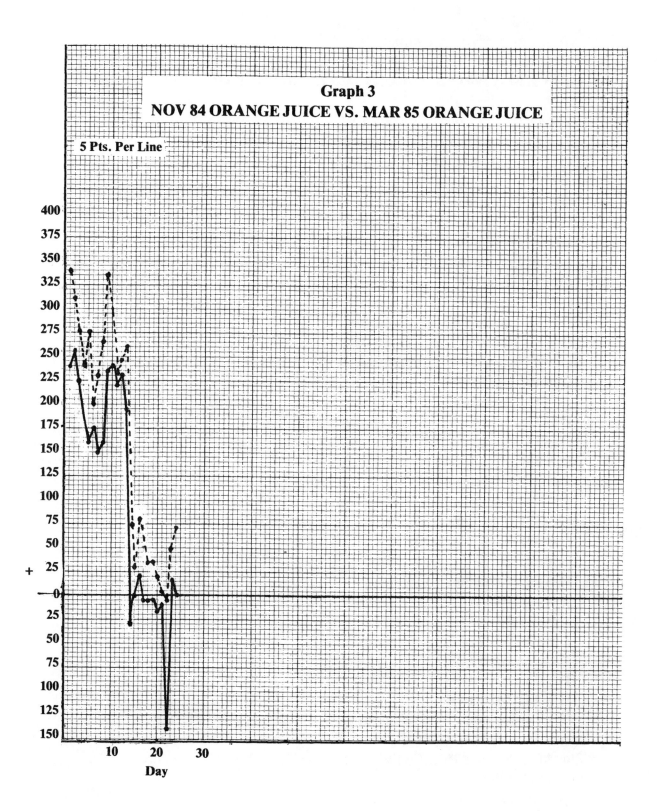

Graph 3
NOV 84 ORANGE JUICE VS. MAR 85 ORANGE JUICE

5 Pts. Per Line

Day

Twin-Line Spreading Examples

SEPTEMBER 1984 VS. MARCH 1985 EURODOLLAR

Overview

Within a five business week period, the twin-line gave two signals. The first was to put on a bull spread and the second to offset. The result is a fair return on margin of over 40%.

Day 1: Started to graph spread.

Day 2: No action.

Day 3: No action.

Day 4: No action.

Day 5: No action.

Day 6: No action.

Day 7: No action.

Day 8: Twin-line signal to put on a bull spread.

Day 9: Went long September, short March at a plus 59 points.

Day 10: No action.

Day 11: No action.

Day 12: No action.

Day 13: No action.

Day 14: No action.

Day 15: No action.

Day 16: No action.

Day 17: No action.

Day 18: No action.

Day 19: No action.

Day 20: No action.

Day 21: No action.

Day 22: No action.

Day 23: No action.

Day 24: No action.

Day 25: No action.

Day 26: No action.

Day 27: Twin-line reversal this day. High went below low price of day 23.

Day 28: Offset at a plus 80 points. Profit 21 points or $525.00. Commission $100.00. Net Profit $424.00. Margin $1,000.00. Return on margin equity: 42½%.

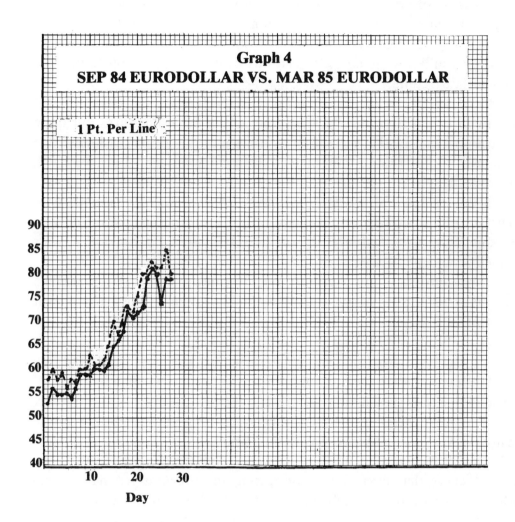

Graph 4
SEP 84 EURODOLLAR VS. MAR 85 EURODOLLAR

1 Pt. Per Line

Day

SPREAD—MARCH/JULY 84 SOYBEANS

The March/July bean spread is a favorite of mine. It is an intra-market spread worthy of your attention. (Please notice that in my description of this spread, I talk a little about the use of mental stops. While twin-line can be completely mechanical, the use of your own mental stops may be something you'll want to consider as a way of injecting your own opinions into twin-line trading).

All too often "How To" books purport to teach readers systems that will make them rich! Unfortunately, the game on the firing line turns out quite differently. It may be that the author assumes a certain degree of knowledge on the part of the reader. I have taken a different approach...I believe it will be to your liking.

I am the teacher and you are the student. No assumption is made with respect to prior knowledge about spreads, so if I seem redundant or harp on the same point over and over again, it is because I do not know your knowledge absorption rate.

The Mar/July graph's scale is in ¼ cent increments. This scale was used so as to make the spread action easily discernible. Usually I use a half cent increment.

(a) On the tenth day (each vertical line contains one day's high and low spread difference), the twin-line graph flashed a signal to put on a bull spread. The solid line (low spread difference) went above a previous high difference (dotted line). We therefore expect Mar. beans to outperform the July beans to the upside. We go long Mar. and short July beans.

The initial mental stop price is at twenty and three-quarter cents. The reason I chose that price is because during the previous ten days, three bottoms at twenty and one-half cents were made. I reasoned that a violation of those bottoms would negate the bullish implications of the spread, and if those lows were violated, I would offset the spread.

Common sense is heightened by experience. As you gain experience, you will think along similar lines. On the eleventh day, the high spread difference was a minus (−) fourteen and one-half cents. The low came in at a minus (−) fifteen and three-quarter cents. Assuming you got the highest difference, your risk would have been about two hundred and seventy-five dollars per spread.

(b) Notice that on the 19th day a very common situation developed. We have the high line above the zero line and the low spread difference below the zero line. As I said, this phenomenon occurs rather frequently. You should not have any difficulty graphing the plus and minus spread difference. At other times, both lines will penetrate on the same day.

(c) We have a reversal on the twin-line graph. What do we do? We play the part of a programmed robot who has instructions to offset using a market order at the opening next day. The price you would have gotten is a minus (−) three cents. That happened to be the high, low and last spread difference for that day. It indicates that beans traded in a very narrow price range all day.

Don't let a high and low spread differential coming in at the same difference throw you into a tizzy with respect to graphing them. Simply draw each line down to the price difference.

Let's recap the situation. We entered a bull spread expecting Mar. beans to gain on the July contract. Our bull signal was correct for that is what happened. We offset the spread at a minus (−) three cents. Our gross profit amounted to eleven and a half cents, or $562.50. Commissions at this writing are $70.00. The margin is $300.00. The profit is $492.50 after commission, or 164.17%!

Would you have actually put on this spread in view of my admonition to wait until you have 30 to 40 days data? Yes, because had you started graphing a few weeks earlier, as I did, you would have taken the signal.

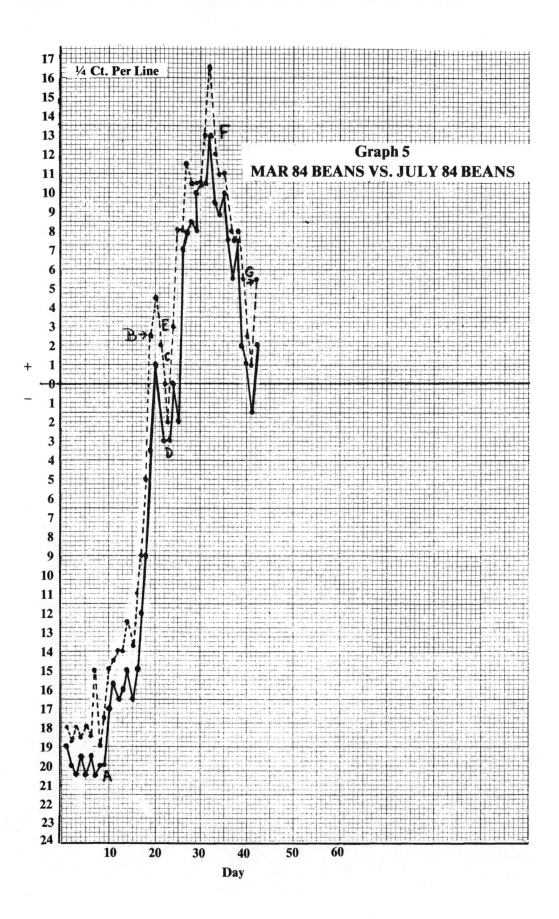

¼ Ct. Per Line

Graph 5
MAR 84 BEANS VS. JULY 84 BEANS

Day

90

THE 84 MARCH VS. JULY BELLY SPREAD

Pork Bellies are extremely volatile and often experience wild price fluctuations. However, if approached cautiously and carefully, large profits can be taken out of the belly spread. Let's look at the PBH84 vs. PBN84 spread (March vs. July).

On day 10, Point A, we get our first bear signal. Next day we go in at the opening shorting March PB and going long the July contract. The fill comes back at +130. A good fill to be sure. The initial stop is 185 or 55 points. Each point is equal to $3.80 so in terms of dollars, we are looking at a $209.00 stop.

Our mental stop is penetrated on day 14 (Point B). The spread is offset on the opening next day using a "market order." We offset at a plus 60. Believe it or not, we made money.

Our original stop was at 130. We offset on a twin-line reversal at 60, so we have a profit of 70 points, or $266.00. Allowing for an $80.00 commission, net profit is $186.00.

The third twin-line signal came in on day 23 (Point C). We place an order to go in at the opening on the next day. Our fill is at 80. The first stop is at 210 points, or 130 points away from the spread difference at which our order was executed. This is equal to $494.00.

We receive a twin-line offsetting signal on day 26 (Point D). Next day we exit the spread at the opening using a market order. The fill is a minus 65. Our loss is 145 points, or $551.00.

A reversal occurred on day 28 (Point E). We go in next day on a bear spread. Our fill is a plus 30. The initial stop is 115 points plus, or 85 points equal to $323.00.

You may have noticed that I did not use a price order to put on the spread. That's because pork bellies are heavily traded. Liquidation or entry is no problem. In addition, the probability of putting on a belly spread is nil if you use a price order due to its volatility.

I have a tendency to write separate buy/sell orders to put on this spread. You will get better fills than if the order is sent in as a spread order. The AE will inform his back office that the two orders represent a spread. This procedure will reduce both commissions for the net positions to a spread commission. Make sure he informs the back office to this effect.

A twin-line reversal occurred on day 32 (Point F). Next day we are out on the opening on a fill of minus 40 points for our second loss. This loss is $228.00 plus $80.00 commission, or a total of $308.00.

A new bear signal came in on day 37 (Point G). We go in on day 38 at the opening at minus 40. The stop is at plus 75 points.

Notice the double arrow around the minus 100 level. The previous low was taken out. The spread looks about ready to fall out of bed!

Day 51 (Point H) produced a twin-line reversal and a trendline penetration. Next day we cover at a minus 160 points. Profit is 120 points, or $456.00.

We did not do very well on the spread. Our net loss is minimal. Had I extended out this spread in point of time, profits would have developed. Regardless, this is a frustrating spread and it should be handled with extreme care.

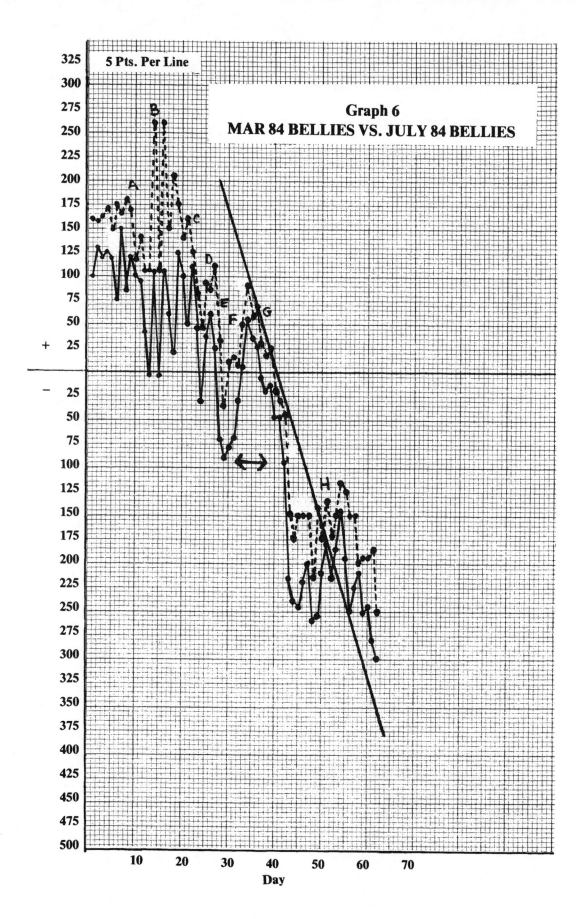

Graph 6
MAR 84 BELLIES VS. JULY 84 BELLIES

5 Pts. Per Line

93

THE DEC 83 VS. DEC 84 T-BILL SPREAD

I want to approach our study of this spread in a somewhat different manner. I would like to treat this spread as a "do-it-yourself" exercise. Letters are used to designate trendlines, twin-line signals, and stop levels. Wherever you see a letter, try and figure out why it has been included.

On day 25 (Point A), a long twin-line signal developed. Next day we go long the 83 Dec. T-Bill contract and go short the 84 Dec. T-Bill contract. Notice the line I drew at Point B. For approximately 14 days, at a range of plus 52 to plus 55, a support line came into being. Thus, we know where our stop should be placed (at a plus 51). If the spread's differential closes (last) at plus 51 or less, we offset next day.

On day 38 (Point C), we have a twin-line offsetting signal. Next day we are out of the position. We do not reverse the spread at this time.

Study the graph to this point in time. Pay particular attention to Point B. Unless this three week support level is taken out, we can only conclude that profit-taking is now going on. It is a good policy to keep in mind that a reversal must have something to reverse. Since the support line (B) is less than 3 weeks old, it is best not to reverse the spread.

On day 42 (Point D), a bullish twin-line signal developed. We go back into the spread next day. Notice how the support line (Point B) held. The stop is at 62 (Point E), one point below the previous reaction. This order becomes a market order, if and only if, the last spread differential hits or goes below the 62 mental stop.

On day 84 (Point F), we exit the spread.

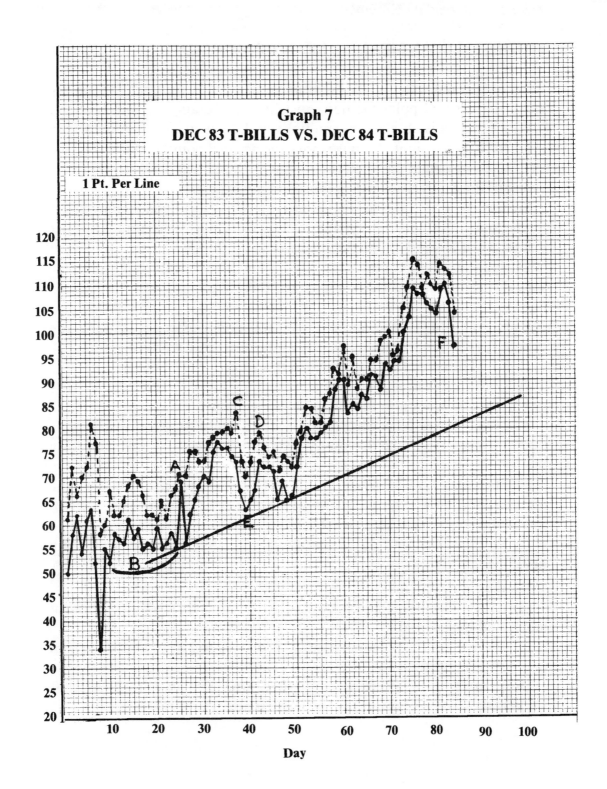

Graph 7
DEC 83 T-BILLS VS. DEC 84 T-BILLS

1 Pt. Per Line

Day

95

THE DEC 83 BEAN MEAL VS. BEAN OIL SPREAD

To obtain the value of the soybean meal futures contract, we simply move the decimal point (as done in Chapter 4 example). The bean oil contract's value is obtained by multiplying the size of the contract by the value in cents per point. Then we move the decimal point all the way to the left. When we obtain the total, the comma is placed two places to the right, giving us the contract's worth in thousands of dollars.

Since there is no room for the oil price in cents per pound, simply insert in the respective columns on the spread work form the total contract values. Then proceed to find the spread dollar difference.

During the almost two months of twin-line graphing for this particular spread, meal remained below oil. Thus, there was no need to use a zero line.

I am going to list the approximate dollar value per trade using the opening price(s) for the following day as the difference received.

It should be noted that I've included this spread in the book because it is a well known spread and because it's a money value spread. I believe it's important you know how to work with money value spreads.

The scale moves from high to low (top to bottom). Meal was weaker than oil, resulting in the downward bias and the need for this particular scaling.

Point A, Day 9, we have our first signal to short the meal and go long the oil. Our stop on a closing (last) basis only is at $3,850.00. The opening spread difference on 8/12/83 was $4,745.00.

At Point B, the 16th day, three points of interest worth mentioning developed:

(1) the short term rally came to an end,

(2) a second twin-line signal was evident allowing the trader to put on an additional spread, and

(3) the mental stop point could now be lowered to $50.00 above the high point of this rally (more on mental stops later).

Drop the stop to $50.00 over Point C (the 20th day) to a price of $7,200.00. That one day pickup was the first after Point B.

At Point D, the 25th day after we began to graph the spread, we get a signal to offset the spread the following day. On the 26th day (Sept. 6, 1983) the opening showed a spread difference of $7,505.00.

On August 12th we put on the spread after a twin-line signal to short the meal and go long the oil. The spread was held for three weeks. We went in at a minus $4,745.00, and closed at a minus $7,505.00 for a profit of $2,760.00. Considering that the original spread margin is about $800.00, we picked up over three times that amount (300%) within a three week period, averaging 100% return per week!

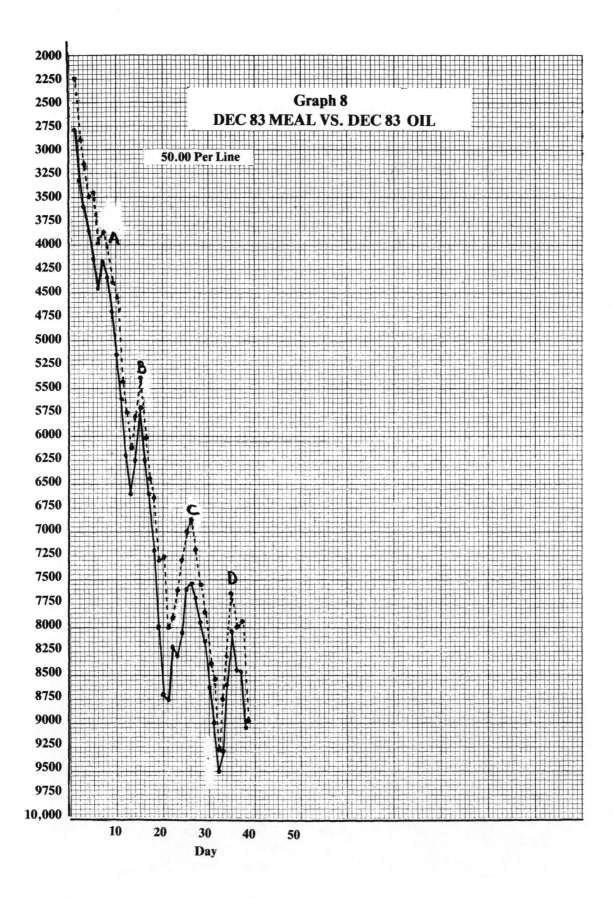

Graph 8
DEC 83 MEAL VS. DEC 83 OIL

50.00 Per Line

98

DEC 83 SWISS FRANC VS DEC 83 D-MARK

For this spread, the twin-line graph is scaled one point per line. The time frame is a 37 day period beginning June 24, 1983.

Point A, the 10th day, is when twin-line signalled a spread trade. On the 11th day, at the opening of trading, we went long the Swiss franc and short the D-mark at a plus 865. Mental stop is at 846, one point below the low.

At Point B (on day 17) we raise the stop to 887, one point below the low of 888.

At Point C (on day 21) the stop is raised to 916, one point below the 917 low.

We have a violation of our stop on the close (Point D, Day 20). We offset the spread on the opening next day. 918 is what we get on the order fill.

The profit is 53 points at $12.50 a point, or a dollar profit value of $662.50, less about an $80.00 brokerage commission.

At Point E we put on a bear spread and the trade is reversed at Point F.

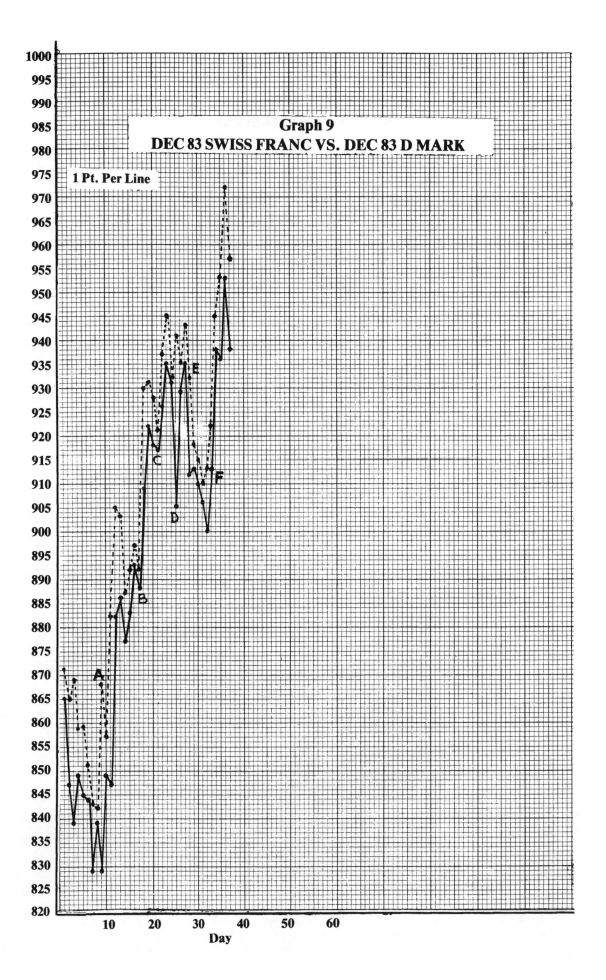

Graph 9
DEC 83 SWISS FRANC VS. DEC 83 D MARK

1 Pt. Per Line

Day

100

DEC 83 T-BONDS VS. DEC 83 GNMA

This spread, as the twin-line shows, is a highly profitable trade. It should be put on using a price order. It has been my experience that the offsetting fills are not too far out of line when a market order is employed.

I want to caution you against a train of thought which you might at sometime entertain. There are some people in the industry who will advise you to offset a spread when the market is moving in the right direction. The right direction meaning the market is moving up when you want to offset a bull spread or lower when offsetting a bear spread. They are incorrect.

When you want out of a position you want out because the twin-line told you to exit the trade. If a stop signal was not hit in the first place, you would have no reason to offset. Obviously a signal to get out may mean trouble if you wait. That is why I strongly recommend you exit a position at the opening using a market order.

For this spread each line has a value of one point, therefore each 32 lines equals a 1% change in the basis, or $1,000.00.

Point A (the 11th day) witnessed our first bear signal to go short the bonds and long the GNMA on a twin-line signal. The opening difference was 6.19. Our stop on a closing basis (last) is 7.03, one point above the previous high. This 16 point stop at $31.25 per point translates to $500.00.

Please note points A, B, C (tops), and D, E, and F (bottoms). You have lower tops and, at point F, both previous bottoms were taken out. It is possible that spread traders put on the same trade the following day at lower prices. The fact remains that the twin-line signal puts you in at 15 or 16 points higher.

At Point G, the 34th day, we get a twin-line reversal signal. Using a market order executed on the following day, we exit the spread. Our offsetting price is 5.13. Our gross profit is 38 points, or $1,187.50. This was accomplished in a 19 day period, thanks to twin-line.

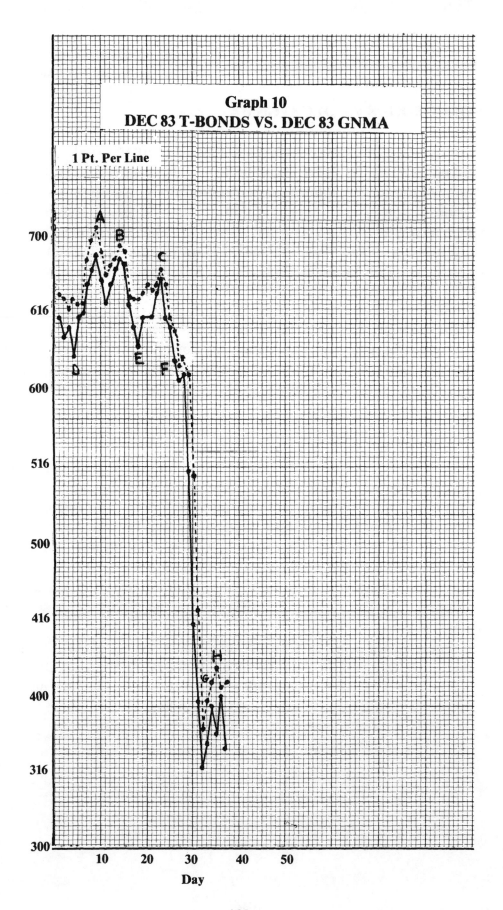

Graph 10
DEC 83 T-BONDS VS. DEC 83 GNMA

1 Pt. Per Line

Day

102

FEB 84 LIVE CATTLE VS. JUNE 84 LIVE CATTLE

Each point move in the cattle spread is equal to $4.00. This spread's range is about 60 points on average. Therefore, an entry order should contain a spread differential amount. Using an entry market order is too risky.

On day 6 (Point A) we have a twin-line bear signal. Next day we short the Feb. live cattle and go long June live cattle at a difference of 312 points. The initial mental stop is 230 points, or $328.00.

Day 10 (Point B) gives us an offsetting signal. Next day we are out of the spread at a spread difference of 185 points. Our loss is $508.00 plus commission of $80.00. A total loss on the trade of $588.00.

Day 16 (Point C) has flashed a new bear signal. Next day we put on another bear spread at a difference of 278 points. The mental stop is 210 points, or $272.00.

On day 33, the stop is lowered to 315 points. A twin-line reversal signal occurred on day 37 (Point D), the spread is offset on day 38 at 300. Profits equalled 112 points or $448.00, less commission of $80.00, resulting in a net profit of $368.00. The loss has been reduced to $220.00.

A bullish reversal occurred on day 43 (Point E) via a twin-line signal. In addition, a trendline was penetrated to the upside. On day 44 we go long the Feb. live cattle and short the June live cattle. We expect the Feb. contract to gain relative to June. The spread difference is a minus 435. Our stop is at minus 480 points, or $225.00.

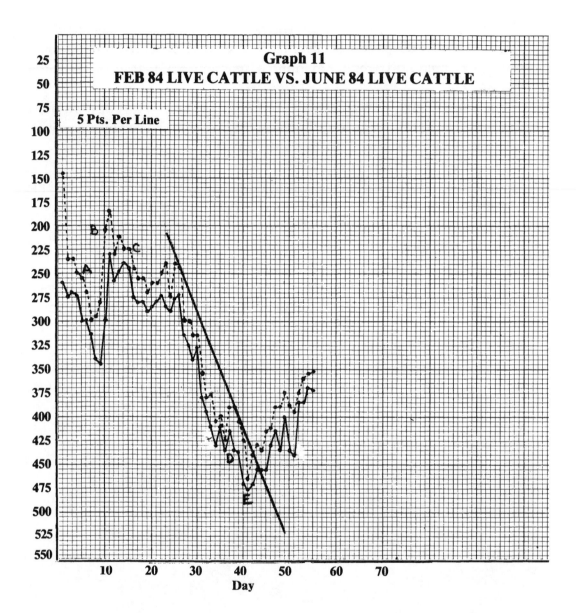

Graph 11
FEB 84 LIVE CATTLE VS. JUNE 84 LIVE CATTLE

5 Pts. Per Line

Day

104

Chapter Ten

A Spread Study—
May 84 Wheat Vs. May 84 Corn

While the twin-line spread program of trading is automatic, a spreader may wish to use actual mental stops. If so, the technique for same will be found in this and the following chapter.

Airplanes, by and large, employ two systems of operation: an automatic system, whereby the aircraft will fly at a set speed, altitude and course (direction). The second system is manual. In this mode, the airplane responds to the decisions of the pilot.

The many, many spread examples in this book attest to the fact that the procedure for putting on or offsetting a position is automatic. No decision is required save for deciding whether or not the spread trader wants to go in in the first place.

Not all traders like or are comfortable with a completely automatic system. I suppose a passenger on a plane would share the same feeling. We prefer that the human element be present. It is for that reason that I have included a manual technique to ascertain where stops should be placed when putting on a spread position. The next two chapters are devoted to manual stop loss evaluation and placement. Just remember, stops are mental. They become actual orders if the stop is hit based on the closing spread difference.

The explanatory format in these two chapters is changed. There is no overview for one thing. I will instead dissect the graph point by point.

What I hope to accomplish is to make you a part of my analysis. Work forms for this spread are found in Chapter 11.

Line A is a trendline which was broken to the downside. This was accomplished with a confirming twin-line sign—a very powerful combination indeed. At this time, I would have gone short wheat and long the corn using a spread market order. My initial stop would be at one-half cent above the high of .9575, on a closing (last price) basis only.

Line B, a second trendline, was penetrated some nine days later. One day after this break a second twin down signal developed. The stop price should have been lowered to one-half cent above the high of the second rally. And a second spread should have been put on using the same stop order.

Anytime you see one twin-line signal confirming a previous signal, you have the makings of a very, very powerful move to follow.

At Point C we lower our stop to one-half cent above the small rally high. Twin-line will give you stop points. Using this method of trading spreads, you do not have to guess where to place a stop.

Point D is a one day rally which failed. You now lower your stop to one-half cent above Point D. This stop includes all positions.

At Point E you go out of all spreads at the market on the opening next day! There are no ands, ifs or buts, about closing out the trade. You have a reversal at this point. The bottom line moved above a previous high point. That is your signal to exit.

There is no way for anyone to know how far the rally can move. If it turns out that we extended the spread too soon, we can always reinstate our position. As it turns out, we will be back in the spread shortly. Regardless, the first rule of trading spreads with profits in mind is to protect capital and accrued profits.

The second reason why the trade must be closed on the opening of the next trading day is because a trendline (letter F) was penetrated to the upside.

You must make it a cardinal rule never to fight the tape...never! Don't rationalize. You cannot assume that the rally is only a little profit taking which is causing the spread to reverse direction. No one knows how long the move is going to last.

Look at Point G, a couple of days after the trade was offset. I inserted two Gs, one above and the second below the previous high to make it easier to follow me. You have a new signal; a twin-line reversal. The high dotted line penetrated the low solid line. The first stop is one-half a cent above the high difference (top letter G).

At Point H, you can relax. The trade should turn out to be more profitable. It took out a previous low difference made eight days before. The spread is very weak which is good for your position.

One other point worth noting is the usual skepticism on the part of many traders to reenter a position. I can only tell you that you will lose profitable trading opportunities if you take that attitude. You trade to make money, pure and simple. If you get a twin-line signal to go back in a position, go back in. Do not deny yourself the benefit of your twin-line signals.

On the 55th day, Point I, you have a reversal. You close out the trade on the next day.

Day 62, Point J, we have a new signal to short the wheat and go long the corn...again. Stop above previous high.

You have your first loss. At Point K the spread reversed and you offset. I drew a line (L) connecting two bottoms. If the spread goes below the trendline, together with a twin-line signal occurring before or slightly after the line (within 3 days), a new bear spread must be put on.

Let's talk about something you already know. No methodology is 100% effective. If it was, there would be no exchange. Everyone would wait for the other trader to act.

Knowledge and acting on that knowledge is not the same thing. Theory is not practice. When everything goes along smoothly, you can become quite content. However, when you have to take a loss (and losses are part of trading), things become more difficult. You do not act because you do not want to take a loss. I am here to tell you that unless rationality overcomes emotionality, don't trade. You are defeated before you begin.

I suffer from the same emotional distate where losses are concerned. Nevertheless, experience overcomes emotions. I will write an offsetting order faster than when I go into a position. I have trained myself to fear a small loss turning into a substantial one. Do the same thing, and the "bottom line" will reflect favorably on your judgement.

Point L, the 67th day, gave another signal to go into the spread. Look at

Point G and Point L. Both are on the high, and both highs are what in technical parlance is called a double top. A double top is a strong resistance level, not easily penetrated.

On the following day we get a trendline penetration. In order of importance you now have: (1) a twin-line signal, (2) a trendline break, and (3) a double top.

The spread has moved to under thirty cents. Our stop is lowered to Point M, placing it one-half cent above the high at .3850. Point M also shows a trendline. If a twin-line reversal occurs we close the trade. We do the same thing if the downsloping trendline is penetrated to the upside.

We have been in and out of the spread a number of times during the previous 13 weeks. All trades were profitable except one.

On day 82, Point N, the spread is offset with another profit on a twin-line reversal coupled with a breaking of the trendline to the upside. I will stop my analysis of the spread at this point. It is suggested you study the rest of the 38 days and see what action you would have taken, and where you would have initiated stop protection. (See next page for critique).

THE SPREAD

It makes absolutely no difference which is the first month of an intra-commodity spread, or which is the first contract in an inter-commodity spread (such as the wheat/corn spread). If the months are reversed, of course the plus/minus signs would be reversed, as would the twin-line graph. Instead of the graph showing a downtrend, there would now be an uptrend showing corn stronger than wheat.

Signals would show the same thing—only reversed. Let me explain. In the wheat vs. corn spread we originally shorted wheat and went long corn, because wheat was weaker than corn and expected to fall faster. However, now if we turn everything upside down and reverse the contract months (doing a corn vs. wheat graph) corn is then expected to fall *less* rapidly than wheat. We will still be going long the corn and short the wheat, however now you're doing it because corn is stronger than wheat (as opposed to saying wheat is weaker relative to corn). The actions taken are still the same, only the semantics are different.

Notice how I scale the May 84 corn vs. wheat graph. It is the exact opposite of the wheat vs. corn scale. While I prefer to use the higher of the commodities first, it makes positively no difference whatsoever which one is first.

With respect to spreads, it does not matter one bit which contract is used to find the difference first. You simply graph it on twin-line, wait for its signals and put on positions.

CRITIQUE

On day 86 you have a bear signal. Using a stop above a previous high would have sufficed. The subsequent fall would have added about eleven hundred dollars.

No spread has seen its high until its high is a matter of record. You never know how far a move will carry. That is why you should act on twin-line signals coldly and unemotionally. It is to your benefit.

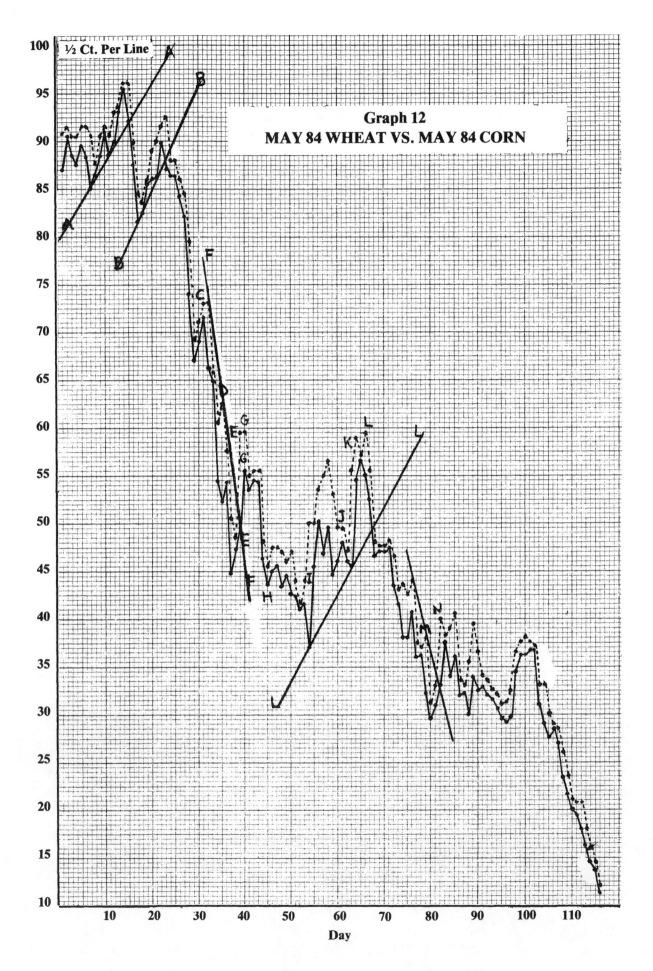

½ Ct. Per Line

Graph 12
MAY 84 WHEAT VS. MAY 84 CORN

Day

110

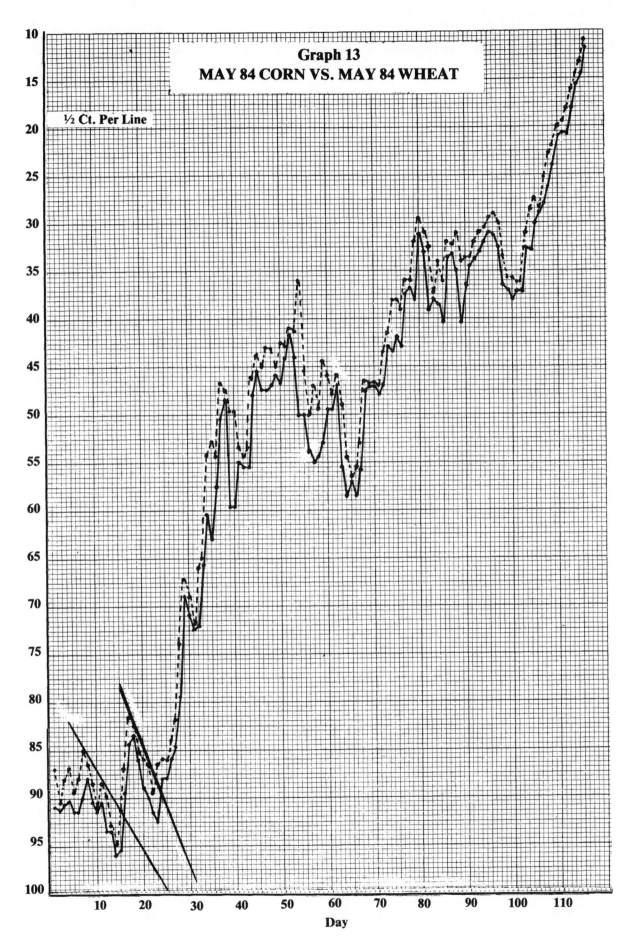

Graph 13
MAY 84 CORN VS. MAY 84 WHEAT

½ Ct. Per Line

Day

Chapter Eleven

Spread Intuition

Intuition in this writer's opinion is the result of a combination of impacts, a few of which can be identified and cultivated. Knowledge and experience are probably the two most important ones.

Another word for intuition is "feel." A subconscious affirmation that what you are doing is the right thing. It is that area, applied to spread trading, that we will be studying. I call that ability "the edge."

To develop a spread trading "feel," we must turn our attention to the data contained on the spread work form—giving life where none existed. Making those numbers talk.

The May 84 wheat and corn form will be our learning center. It contains 116 days of data. I have taken the liberty of numbering each day so as to make reference days easier to find.

You should know the directional movement of a spread during the 6 to 8 weeks prior to acting on a twin-line signal. Was the spread moving in a sideways action? If so, it is not ready for trading. Why tie up margin in a spread moving within narrow parameters. Many spreads trade within a narrow range for months on end before moving decisively in one direction or the other.

To develop a greater "feel" about a spread, you should ask yourself three questions: (1) What was the previous major trend?, (2) What is the present trend?, and (3) What may be the next trend? To develop our feeling about this particular spread, I will address each question individually.

Spread Intuition

What was the previous major trend? Defining a major trend borders on a subjective evaluation. If the trend was in progress for a number of weeks or months, accompanied by a large swing in spread values, you can assume that was a major trend.

What is the present trend? If the spread is moving in a sideways action, there is no trend. It may just be resting preparatory to resuming its previous trend, or it may be gathering strength (being accumulated) and about to be reversing direction. This brings us to the third question.

What may be the next trend? First, let me ask you a question. What is the month in which you are attempting to get a handle on the probable direction of the spread? Suppose you are two months away from a monthly turning point (MTP), what might ensue between now and then in the spread? It would be fair to say that the spread, while in a sideways action now, will probably turn down going into the MTP.

The spread might also continue its non-directional pattern going into the MTP. The conclusion; the spread is in a sideways movement with a probable downward bias developing over the next couple of months. Therefore, I just watch it for a while longer and see what unfolds.

Assuming this month is a MTP time, how would you think about the spread? Since the spread is non-directional at the moment, you might consider this action as a prelude to a change in direction. After all, the previous trend has changed to a sideways action. In addition, you are in a seasonal period in which the spread has changed direction.

Is there anything else you can learn at this time about the spread? You bet there is! Knowing that the signs point to higher spread differences, you begin to "eye-ball" the twin-line graph in earnest, looking for these signs:

1. During the sideways action, what is the high side and what has been the low side of the spread?

2. Mentally draw an upper and lower line encapsulating the high/low parameters.

3. How often has the spread difference touched the top line before turning down and vice-versa?

4. What is the penetration spread difference over the imaginary top line?

Do you know what you are accomplishing to this point in time? You are developing a feel about the spread. What has transpired is all in your head. The situations I posed and the questions I asked will be going through your mind as you scan your work.

Let us now turn to page one of the work form in an effort to heighten our sensitivity about the spread, and at the same time, sharpening our awareness of what may ensue.

During the first 14 days since we began to graph wheat vs. corn, the recorded action confirms the twin-line graph. The spread differences are telling us little about the next trend. We do see that two prices stand out as the high and low spread difference for the time frame—a low spread difference of plus eighty-six and three quarter cents was recorded on Day 8 and it is still holding.

First assumption: the spread difference recorded on Day 8 may be a support because to this point in time it has not been violated.

Second assumption: if this low is violated, a bear spread trade should be considered. The rationale is based on a violation of a support line. This difference was recorded in the 'high' column on the form.

Day 14 was the date on which the highest spread differential was reached at ninety-five and a quarter cents. The spread is moving within an eleven cent ($550.00) range.

Assumption one: If the spread can penetrate the high difference, a bull spread is in order.

Day 17 tells us the story. The spread difference violated the previous low of plus .86754. We should consider going short the wheat and long the corn. We have an indication that the wheat contract should lose more relative to corn (fall faster). Incidentally, take a glance at day 116. The spread narrowed to plus .1125, a seventy-three cent difference from our first signal. The profit amounted to over thirty-six hundred ($3,600.00) dollars per spread during a five month period.

These exercises are designed to increase a commonality between you and your work. In time you will be able to simply look at a form and quickly spot the strength and weakness of the spread subconsciously.

There is no way I can prove to you that intuition (feel) is a real phenomenon and gives one who cultivates it a major edge. I can only tell you that it exists. You would do well to begin now to evaluate twin-line graphs subjectively.

DAY 23 SHOWS A RALLY WITH A FAILURE

After putting on the bear spread a day after the bear signal (day 17), a rally

115

ensued which failed to penetrate the high point. Day 28 reinforces the bear signal when it plunged to a new low.

Through constant visual graph study, your "sixth" sense will become sharply honed.

June 1, 83

MAY 84 WHEAT VS MAY 84 CORN

	WHEAT HIGH	CORN HIGH	DIFF HIGH	WHEAT LOW	CORN LOW	DIFF LOW	WHEAT LAST	CORN LAST	DIFF LAST
1	38425	29725	+.8700	38025	29225	+.8800	38350	29275	+.9075
2	38775	29650	+.9125	38400	29350	+.9050	38775	29650	+.9125
3	38800	29750	+.9050	38525	29575	+.8950	38525	29700	+.8825
4	38650	29925	+.8725	38475	29525	+.8950	38625	29600	+.9025
5	38700	29550	+.9150	38500	29350	+.9150	38500	29550	+.8950
6	38400	29400	+.9000	38025	29200	+.8825	38400	29250	+.9150
7	38400	29375	+.9025	37700	29200	+.8500	37900	29300	+.8600
8	37950	29275	+.8675	37775	29075	+.8700	37850	29100	+.8750
9	37975	29125	+.8850	37725	28700	+.9025	37975	28925	+.9050
10	38150	29050	+.9100	37850	28700	+.9150	37875	28750	+.9125
11	37950	28900	+.9050	37700	28700	+.9000	37700	28850	+.8850
12	38400	29075	+.9325	37900	28900	+.9000	38350	29050	+.9300
13	38475	29125	+.9350	38225	28900	+.9325	38275	28925	+.9350
14	38425	28900	+.9525	38200	28625	+.9575	38300	28725	+.9575
15	38550	29375	+.9175	38300	28750	+.9550	38550	29375	+.9175
16	38750	29800	+.8950	38425	29525	+.8900	38550	29800	+.8750
17	38600	30150	+.8450	38250	29800	+.8450	38300	30150	+.8150
18	38475	30150	+.8325	38200	29900	+.8300	38250	30000	+.8250
19	38175	29525	+.8600	37675	29150	+.8525	37775	29175	+.8600
20	38075	29200	+.8875	37575	28975	+.8600	38000	29100	+.8900
21	38175	29175	+.9000	37600	28950	+.8650	37725	29100	+.8625
22	38600	29450	+.9150	37950	28925	+.9025	37950	28975	+.8975
23	38225	28975	+.9250	37400	28675	+.8725	37525	28850	+.8675
24	37525	28725	+.8800	37250	28500	+.8750	37250	28625	+.8625
25	37950	29325	+.8625	37500	28700	+.8800	37950	29300	+.8650
26	37950	29425	+.8525	37675	29100	+.8575	37700	29275	+.8425
27	37575	29150	+.8425	37325	29025	+.8300	37525	29150	+.8175
28	38100	30150	+.7950	37550	29700	+.7870	37550	30150	+.7400
29	37700	30950	+.6750	37375	30500	+.6875	37400	30625	+.6775

MAY 84 WHEAT VS MAY 84 CORN

	WHEAT HIGH	CORN HIGH	DIFF HIGH	WHEAT LOW	CORN LOW	DIFF LOW	WHEAT LAST	CORN LAST	DIFF LAST
30	37775	30750	+.7025	37400	30300	+.7100	37525	30625	+.6900
31	37900	30625	+.7275	37500	30350	+.7150	37500	30375	+.7125
32	37775	31150	+.6625	37550	30350	+.7200	37775	31025	+.6750
33	38200	31700	+.6500	38000	31450	+.6550	38100	31625	+.6475
34	38250	32475	+.5775	37850	31800	+.6050	37925	32475	+.5450
35	39700	33475	+.6225	38325	33050	+.5275	39525	33475	+.6050
36	40125	34475	+.5650	38800	33050	+.5750	39325	33875	+.5450
37	39750	34700	+.5050	39175	34200	+.4975	39175	34700	+.4475
38	39050	34200	+.4850	38450	33700	+.4750	39000	34200	+.4800
39	39500	34550	+.4950	38950	33300	+.5650	39325	33350	+.5975
40	39250	33625	+.5625	39125	33150	+.5975	39150	33600	+.5550
41	39925	34550	+.5375	39600	34100	+.5500	39875	34525	+.5350
42	39850	34400	+.5450	39475	34000	+.5475	39800	34250	+.5550
43	40500	35100	+.5400	39700	34150	+.5550	40400	35075	+.5325
44	40450	35650	+.4800	39875	35250	+.4625	39900	35275	+.4625
45	40350	35975	+.4375	39700	35150	+.4550	40225	35800	+.4425
46	40350	35850	+.4500	39925	35150	+.4775	40025	35300	+.4725
47	40600	36050	+.4550	39850	35100	+.4750	40175	35900	+.4275
48	40500	36150	+.4350	39900	35200	+.4700	40025	35700	+.4325
49	40325	35875	+.4450	40050	35475	+.4575	40150	35700	+.4450
50	41375	36700	+.4675	40250	36000	+.4250	41050	36700	+.4350
51	41175	36900	+.4275	40825	36400	+.4425	40875	36600	+.4275
52	41125	37025	+.4100	40475	36350	+.4125	40800	36675	+.4125
53	42100	37675	+.4425	41050	36900	+.4150	42100	37675	+.4425
54	43650	38675	+.4975	40700	37100	+.3600	41950	37525	+.4425
55	42300	37750	+.4550	41625	36850	+.4775	42000	37025	+.4975
56	42150	36850	+.5300	41050	36025	+.5025	41550	36200	+.5350
57	41800	36800	+.5000	41300	35800	+.5500	41475	36800	+.4675
58	43475	37800	+.5675	42750	37800	+.4950	43475	37800	+.5675

MAY 84 WHEAT VS MAY 84 CORN

	WHEAT HIGH	CORN HIGH	DIFF HIGH	WHEAT LOW	CORN LOW	DIFF LOW	WHEAT LAST	CORN LAST	DIFF LAST
59	44100	38800	+.5300	42700	38250	+.4450	42850	38375	+.4475
60	43350	38400	+.4950	42500	37900	+.4660	42800	38125	+.4675
61	43800	39000	+.4800	42650	37700	+.4950	42725	37825	+.4900
62	42950	38325	+.4625	42200	37500	+.4700	42950	38325	+.4625
63	43500	38275	+.5225	42550	37600	+.4950	43150	37600	+.5550
64	43050	37275	+.5775	42050	36600	+.5450	42475	36600	+.5875
65	43150	37475	+.5675	42300	36600	+.5700	43125	37450	+.5675
66	43200	37700	+.5500	42100	36450	+.5650	42625	36650	+.5975
67	42900	37350	+.5550	42350	36850	+.5500	42550	37325	+.5225
68	42700	37925	+.4775	42150	37500	+.4650	42500	37850	+.4650
69	42700	38000	+.4700	42275	37550	+.4725	42375	37675	+.4700
70	42500	37800	+.4700	42100	37375	+.4725	42500	37775	+.4725
71	43000	38275	+.4725	42700	37975	+.4725	42825	38050	+4775
72	42700	38025	+.4675	42200	37850	+.4350	42350	37925	+.4425
73	42750	38550	+.4200	41300	37000	+.4300	41300	37150	+.4150
74	41450	37100	+.4350	40800	36600	+.4200	40800	36975	+.3825
75	41050	37250	+.3800	40100	35975	+.4125	40200	35975	+.4225
76	40650	36575	+4075	40100	35700	+.4400	40450	36525	+.3925
77	41050	37375	+.3675	40500	36750	+.3750	40950	37350	+.3600
78	41000	37325	+.3675	40475	36850	+.3625	40675	37025	+.3650
79	41850	38025	+.3825	41250	37950	+.3300	41250	38025	+.3225
80	40800	37850	+.2950	40250	37125	+.3125	40275	37150	+.3125
81	40350	37050	+.3300	39375	36250	+.3125	39625	36400	+.3225
82	39650	36375	+.3275	39025	35475	+.3550	39600	35675	+3925
83	39875	36125	+.3750	39500	35750	+.3750	39825	36025	+.3800
84	39875	36450	+.3425	39200	35300	+.3900	39200	35350	+.3850
85	39100	35400	+.3700	38600	34550	+.4050	39000	35375	+.3625
86	39250	35900	+.3350	38700	35450	+.3250	39050	35850	+.3200
87	39050	35825	+.3225	38650	35425	+.3225	39050	35750	+.3300

119

MAY 84 WHEAT VS MAY 84 CORN

	WHEAT HIGH	CORN HIGH	DIFF HIGH	WHEAT LOW	CORN LOW	DIFF LOW	WHEAT LAST	CORN LAST	DIFF LAST
88	39025	35950	+3075	38750	35225	+.3525	38775	35250	+.3525
89	38900	35500	+.3400	38900	34850	+.4050	38900	35475	+.3425
90	39250	35975	+.3275	39100	35450	+.3650	39125	35725	+.3400
91	39150	35725	+3425	38575	35275	+.3300	38700	35300	+.3400
92	38550	35200	+.3350	38100	34825	+.3275	38375	35175	+.3200
93	38450	35250	+.3200	38200	34950	+.3250	38250	35125	+.3125
94	38225	35025	+.3200	37925	34875	+.3050	37950	34900	+.3050
95	38600	35500	+.3100	38150	35125	+.3025	38375	35450	+.2925
96	38450	35550	+.2900	38250	35150	+.3100	38350	35225	+.3125
97	38400	35425	+.2975	38025	35025	+.3000	38350	35075	+.3275
98	38700	35175	+.3525	38275	34925	+.3350	38650	35025	+.3625
99	38625	35000	+.3625	38300	34600	+.3700	38350	34625	+.3725
100	38300	34475	+.3825	37550	33800	+.3750	37600	33975	+.3625
101	37975	34300	+.3675	37475	33800	+.3675	37875	34150	+.3725
102	37875	34175	+.3700	37575	33900	+.3875	37600	33925	+.3675
103	38100	34850	+.3250	37800	34550	+.3250	37800	34700	+.3100
104	37900	34625	+.3275	36700	33825	+.2875	37150	33950	+.3200
105	37225	34275	+.2950	36475	33700	+.2775	36975	34000	+.2975
106	37200	34300	+.2900	36950	34050	+.2900	37150	34175	+.2875
107	37250	34425	+.2825	36750	34050	+.2700	36950	34125	+.2825
108	36950	34350	+.2600	36450	34125	+.2325	36700	34225	+.2475
109	36975	34800	+.2175	36750	34425	+.2325	36875	34675	+.2200
110	36950	34850	+.2100	36475	34450	+.2025	36900	34800	+.2100
111	37250	35225	+.2025	36825	34850	+.1975	37225	35150	+.2075
112	37500	35675	+.1825	37150	35075	+.2075	37475	35675	+.1800
113	37550	35925	+.1625	37300	35500	+.1800	37525	35900	+.1625
114	37600	36150	+.1450	37375	35800	+.1575	37375	35850	+.1525
115	37325	35875	+.1450	37050	35700	+.1350	37225	35850	+.1375
116	37125	36000	+.1125	36575	35400	+.1175	36625	35500	+.1125

120

Chapter Twelve

High And Low Spread Months

Do not accept the information contained herein as sacroscant. Let the market prove itself. The volatility and character of spreads do change. It behooves you to keep an "open" mind, especially when you are anticipating a high or low month during which time the spread is expected to change direction.

We live in a fluid world. Times change as well as our precepts. Certain investment vehicles which are considered "wise investments" for long stretches at a time, do turn down in their trading cycle. Likewise, certain bad investments can suddenly turn good. For example, utility companies, once out of favor, have become quite strong in recent times.

In the futures business, some commodities which were once highly traded have seen their volume reduced to almost nothing. Egg and potato contracts are fine examples.

The point of all this is for you to be cognizant of change. Historical data is not a basis on which to take a position. It is only a gauge of what happened in the past. While history tends to repeat, it rarely does so in precisely the same way or in the same month.

The high and low months in which a spread has crested or made its trough usually vary from year to year. Sometimes the spread comes in "right on the money," while at other times the spread will totally disregard its seasonal characteristics.

121

In addition, some spreads make more than one high or low during a year. When this situation occurs, you will probably get more than one twin-line signal. For example, you may have put on a bull spread only to see a reversal occur within a few weeks. Soon you may get another signal indicating you should put on a spread going the other way. This should not hurt you much, if at all, because of the very unique stop rules twin-line utilizes. You may even come out of this potentially perilous situation with a profit. In spread trading, or any form of investing, keep an open mind. When you see a change...you change.

If a spread moves in contra-seasonal fashion, get on it in line with its present trend as soon as you receive a twin-line signal. Contra-seasonal moves occur when fundamentals influencing the spread are present; influences which may not be readily discernible to the trader.

Following is a table of expected high months and low months for a number of intra-commodity spreads. This information can be used to supplement your twin-line work:

INTRA-COMMODITY SPREADS

Spread	High Months	Low Months
Corn	Oct. - Nov.	May
Wheat	August	Oct.
Oats	Oct.	Aug.
Beans	Aug. - Oct.	July - Nov.
Bean Meal	Sept.	July
Bean Oil	Aug.	Oct.
Feeder Cattle	May	Sept.
Live Cattle	Oct.	Aug.
Live Hogs	June	Sept.
Pork Bellies	July	Sept.
Cotton	Aug.	Oct.
Sugar	June	Oct.
Coffee	Oct.	June
Orange Juice	March	Nov. - Dec.
Currencies	Sufficient data not avail.	
Financial Instr.	Sufficient data not avail.	
Lumber	May	Nov.
Plywood	June	Nov.
Stock Indexes	Sufficient data not avail.	
Heating Oil	Oct.	June
Platinum	Sept.	Dec.
Gold	Nov.	Aug.
Silver	Jan.	Oct.

122

I cannot stress too strongly the fact that high and low month data does not always run true to form. As a matter of fact, different trading months may exhibit different high and low time frames. After all is said and done, let your twin-line work be your guide.

I have decided not to include high-low months for inter-commodity spreads as well as the inter-exchange spreads because the data is too misleading. Use twin-line signals and do not concern yourself with inter-market spread high and low monthly turning points.

The number of spread trading possibilities runs into the hundreds. In devising spreads, two factors must be considered: (1) the contracts comprising the spread must somehow be related (for example, you would not spread orange juice and wheat, or silver and plywood), (2) the second factor has to do with liquidity. If the OI (Open Interest) is below 3500 on any contract forming a spread, regardless of a twin-line signal, do *not* put on the spread. If the liquidity isn't there—neither are you!

Chapter Thirteen

Hedging Using Twin-Line Graphs

While it is highly unlikely that a large number of readers of this book do any professional hedging of the actuals, I would be remiss if I did not include some general twin-line hedging information for those who do undertake hedging strategies. Let's begin by understanding the few terms unique to hedging.

Q: What are actuals?

A: Actuals are the physical control (inventory) of a commodity, or the use and/or conversion of a commodity at some point in time. Examples include a farmer who owns and controls his crop, or a cereal manufacturer who has a need for a crop, or an international company concerned about converting (exchanging) foreign currency into the currency of another country.

Q: What is hedging?

A: Hedging is designed to insure "price" protection as much as possible by usually taking trades opposite to one's market position.

Q: What is a hedger?

A: A hedger is anyone who owns, or has a soon to be vested interest in buying, selling or converting a commodity.

Q: What is a basis chart?

A: A basis chart depicts the difference between the cash price and the futures price (above and below a zero line). The basis chart is similar to the spread chart. The only difference is that you are using the daily cash price vs. the last price of the nearest contract month, as compared to using two futures contracts to obtain the spread differential.

Since the basis chart is composed of one line depicting the cash vs. contract price, it is one dimensional and has serious limitations for developing hedging strategies. This notion is supported by the less than favorable results American multinational companies have reported in their currency hedging transactions using the one dimensional charts. My twin-line graph will (due to its two dimensional nature), I believe, give American multinational companies an edge in their future hedging undertakings.

Q: What is meant by price protection?

A: This concept is best illustrated by a few examples. Suppose a farmer has obligated himself to sell his soon to be harvested crop in September. The farmer agrees to turn over the crop at the then cash price. Basically the farmer has one major concern. Will the cash price in September be high enough to result in offsetting all his costs plus a reasonable profit? The farmer knows the price he will have to receive to cover his expenses plus a profit. To protect himself, he will go into the futures markets and short the September contract.

Either way the September contract moves, the farmer is protected. If, for example, the corn contract moves higher as the cash price moves higher, he will gain on the cash price advance while losing on his short position. The difference may be a little more or less than he anticipated but he did protect his cost plus profit by taking approximately an equal (but opposite) position to the amount of corn he agreed to sell in the futures market. (This admittedly is a very simplistic example and is only presented here for those with just a passing interest in the hedging concept).

When a hedger owns the commodity and seeks price protection by going short in the market, the hedger is said to be long the basis. Since the farmer wants to protect his investment against "falling" prices, he will short the market.

The user of the corn (assuming the user is a cereal company), is faced with an opposite problem to that of the farmer. Whereas the farmer is concerned about a lower cash price at the time of delivery, the user is worried about the cash price being higher.

The user will go long (buy) the September corn contract. If the corn price falls, the user will lose on his long position, but offset that loss by paying a smaller cash price. The user is said to be "short the basis."

The cattle rancher, hog raiser or your local loan officer faces similar concerns in their respective businesses. They will go into the meat and financial instruments markets to hedge against lower cash prices or interest rates. In fact, the primary function of a futures exchange is to serve the many industries who need to hedge in order to secure some degree of price protection.

The multinational corporation needs to protect itself from disquieting foreign currency exchange differences brought about through changing political, economic and military climates. Without effective hedging strategies (and I stress the word "effective,") the international company is at the mercy of these unpredictable forces.

The central questions regarding currency exchange protection is how to do it and what tools should be employed? With minor adjustments, the twin-line spreading method I've presented you with can be utilized in hedging situations. The twin-line graph as it applies to currency hedging will illuminate trend direction in bold relief. A penetration of a twin-line trendline must be strictly followed. Twin-line signals must be addressed in the same manner as when found in spreads.

To do a twin-line graph for the purpose of devising hedging strategies requires that you have access to "cash" data, as well as the high, low and last price of the nearest contract month.

The work form will show cash vs. the currency in all three columns. To obtain the highest and lowest basis difference, proceed in the same manner as you would were you looking for the respective spread differentials. Plot the spread in the same manner discussed earlier. Of course, you would offset as the spot month aproaches and roll the positions over onto the next contract month.

Chapter 14

Additional Topics

SPREAD PORTFOLIO MANAGEMENT

To some, portfolio management is the art of spreading risk, or risk diversification. I find the most critical area in managing a portfolio based on the twin-line trading concept to be much different. Rather than risk diversification I find it most important to concentrate on profit maximization. In other words, rather than concentrating on various techniques (however sound they may be) to minimize risk, I find it more beneficial to focus my efforts on techniques to maximize my profits.

My research into maximizing spread portfolios is composed of:

1. Bull and bear spread positions.
2. Different commodity family spreads.
3. Intra and inter futures spreads.
4. 70% maximum capital deployment.
5. Adding to positions when accrued profits are 30% of initial margin requirements.
6. Stop Order protection (as outlined in Chapter 8).

TWIN-LINE AND COMMODITY OPTIONS

Just as bull or bear signals will develop on twin-line spread graphs, so too will twin-line signals manifest themselves in spreading commodity options.

The same precautions apply in options spreading as detailed for futures contracts: (1) the option *must* be listed for trading on a futures exchange, (2) sufficient liquidity must be present so as to enter and exit a spread without giving up too much in the way of price. *Always* ask the AE to get you a "floor" quote, (3) do not (I repeat) do not trade options through a bullion dealer. Their high commissions will negate any real chance to profit. Listed options are the only way to go if your goals are protection and profits.

Use your own discretion in valuing twin-line options scales. It is a good idea to run two different scales at first before deciding which one is preferable.

It is best to work with options which have a remaining life of at least six months.

Do not hold an option going into the last month of its life. At this time there are options on only a few of the futures families. However, new option contracts are being introduced frequently, so additional spread trading option opportunities will increase.

Please drop me a line if you have any problems trading options via my twin-line methodology and I will help set you on course.

Also, please contact me for information regarding my book *"Advanced Profitable Futures Options Trading Using Simple Arithmetic."*

TWIN-LINE COMPUTER PROGRAMS

If you own or can secure either the HP-41C, CV or CX calculators, you can purchase a program to automatically give you a spread's high and low differential simply by pressing a few buttons. There is no limit as to the amount or variety of spreads you can do each day in a fraction of the time it would take you to just post the prices on the spread work form. This includes futures option spreads.

Please write or call:

Lambert Programming Service
434 N. Crescent Heights Blvd.
Los Angeles, CA 90048
Telephone: 1-(213)-658-MATH

The Twin-Line Spread Graph is available as a software package for the IBM and requires no computer or commodity experience to utilize. Everything you need to know is on the screen. The advantages of the Twin-Line software are:

1. Any spread can be on the monitor in seconds.
2. Literally hundreds of spreads can be checked.
3. All spreads are two dimensional.
4. Spread Alert. An audio alert sounds when a Twin-Line signal develops, a Twin-Line trend penetration begins or both types of signals are taking place.
5. Each day the spread difference is automatically updated.
6. Automatic or manual spread graph scaling. The computer will automatically scale a spread or you can substitute different scale values.
7. Point differences (including T-Bonds, GNMA's and money spreads) are automatically computed.
8. Flexible time frames allow you to track as many days as you would like.
9. Specially written booklet on maximizing your trading through this program.

For information about the program, contact:

Lambert Programming Service
434 N. Crescent Heights Blvd.
Los Angeles, CA 90048
Telephone: 1-(213)-658-MATH

The Twin-Line software program can be used with a number of data retrieval vendors. Instructions are included in the software package for manually updating your data banks.

Conclusion

Albert Einstein was once asked how he would proceed to solve a problem within a ten minute time frame. His answer was that he would think about it for the first nine minutes.

In terms of mastering the difficult problem of becoming a consistently profitable spread trader, this twin-line spread trading course can be considered your "nine minutes." The application and implementation of what you have learned will assist you immensely in your future spread trading in minute 10 and beyond.

My best wishes for twin-line profits go with you.